Creative Work Beyond Precarity

This book offers an original critical evaluation of how freelance careers can be established and sustained in the increasingly uncertain global creative economy.

Developing from the author's theoretical and empirical research at the nexus of precarious work and entrepreneurial learning, it provides an in-depth understanding of why and how creatives can learn to become entrepreneurial and how this relates to creative entrepreneurship. This book traces how arts work became creative labour and explores the contemporary organisation of artistic and creative practices to understand practical alternatives to the individualised careers we currently feel responsible for maintaining. Inspired particularly by the work of Raymond Williams, creative work is reconceptualised as practice-based collaborative learning encounters through which we might put shared feelings of precarity to work towards the production and practice of alternative possibilities.

Accessible and concise, breaking down complex concepts through practical examples and linking the creative process to entrepreneurial learning, this book will be of interest to students, educators and researchers studying and working in the creative economy.

Tim Butcher is Associate Professor of Organisation Studies at the University of Tasmania, Australia.

Routledge Focus on the Global Creative Economy
Series Editor: Aleksandar Brkić
Goldsmiths, University of London, UK

This innovative Shortform book series aims to provoke and inspire new ways of thinking, new interpretations, emerging research, and insights from different fields. In rethinking the relationship of creative economies and societies beyond the traditional frameworks, the series is intentionally inclusive. Featuring diverse voices from around the world, books in the series bridge scholarship and practice across arts and cultural management, the creative industries and the global creative economy.

Cultural Mediation for Museums
Driving Audience Engagement
Edited by Michela Addis, Isabella de Stefano and Valeria Guerrisi

Rethinking Cultural Centers
A Nordic Perspective on Multipurpose Cultural Organizations
Tomas Järvinen

Curating, Interpretation and Museums
When Attitude Becomes Form
Sylvia Lahav

Contemporary Exhibition-Making and Management
Curating IMT Gallery as a Hybrid Space
Mark Rohtmaa-Jackson

Digitization and Culture in Vietnam
Emma Duester

Creative Work Beyond Precarity
Learning to Work Together
Tim Butcher

For more information about this series, please visit: www.routledge.com/Routledge-Focus-on-the-Global-Creative-Economy/book-series/RFGCE

Creative Work Beyond Precarity

Learning to Work Together

Tim Butcher

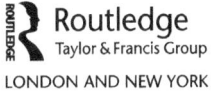
Routledge
Taylor & Francis Group

LONDON AND NEW YORK

First published 2023
by Routledge
4 Park Square, Milton Park, Abingdon, Oxon OX14 4RN

and by Routledge
605 Third Avenue, New York, NY 10158

Routledge is an imprint of the Taylor & Francis Group, an informa business

© 2023 Tim Butcher

British Library Cataloguing-in-Publication Data
A catalogue record for this book is available from the British Library

ISBN: 978-0-367-75326-9 (hbk)
ISBN: 978-0-367-75329-0 (pbk)
ISBN: 978-1-003-16202-5 (ebk)

DOI: 10.4324/9781003162025

Typeset in Times New Roman
by Apex CoVantage, LLC

Contents

vi *Contents*

Acknowledgements

This book is the outcome of a desire to learn how to work more creatively. I am fortunate to have collaborated with and been guided by many generous people who have shared with me how and why they do creative work. Through my research, I have gained insight into not only what creative work is today and how precarious it can feel, but also what hope it provides for the future.

Thank you firstly to the coworkers, arts workers and artists who shared their working lives with me. In particular, I am grateful to Selina, Bern, Richard, Rachel, Isabel, Helena and Farhad; whose stories feature in this book, and all *Tales of Precarity* project participants. Thank you also to friends and collaborators at Hub Australia, Impact Hub, RMIT University, Counterpoints Arts, The Open University and the Tate. Without your support and collegiality, this book would not have been possible. Special mention must go to Áine and Dijana – your work is phenomenal.

I'd also like to thank my many academic colleagues who have provided the inspiration, advice and support that have culminated in this monograph. Thank you especially to Ann and Steve for reviewing the final draft. And Martyna, Barry, Peter, George and José Rodrigo, I am more grateful to you than you may ever know.

My gratitude also to the team at Routledge for your patience and encouragement. Terry and Jacqueline, I really appreciate you giving me the time to produce something meaningful. Alex, thank for your astute editorial guidance, and Naomi, thank you for your editorial support.

Thanks too to Bea and Deborah for listening. And a huge thank you to Jen and Beth for your love and support.

Finally, thank you to the University of Tasmania for giving me the time and space to write this book.

1 Creative work

An introduction

Creative freedom

> Culture is ordinary. An interest in learning or the arts is simple, pleasant and natural. A desire to know what is best, and to do what is good, is the whole positive nature of man [sic].
>
> (Williams, 1958/1989, p. 7)

Culture is ordinary, but is it as straightforward as Raymond Williams suggested in 1958? Contemporary cultural production and consumption come in many forms in the creative economy. In various ways, it has made art more accessible, cultural consumption more inclusive and created new forms of work for many. The idea of a creative economy is replete with all-consuming hope and promise. Defined economically, as it is, the creative economy invites us to 'do what is good' for ourselves (and the economy) through the pursuit of creative careers or artistic practices that are intrinsically meaningful to us. When so many other forms of work seem to feel increasingly devoid of meaning, the simple idea of an individual pursuit of creative freedom as a career choice is seductive. The power of creative economy discourse lies in how that simple idea is communicated.

Creative freedom could be viewed as idealistic and bourgeois, not ordinary. In some ways it is. The creative economy promises both liberation from the apparent mundanities of more traditional forms of employment, and freedom to (re)define ourselves through our work. Viewed sociologically, the language and practices of creativity have become entangled in notions of working independently and entrepreneurially for our individualised selves. Yet the supposed freedoms of creative work bring with them risks, responsibilities, uncertainties, insecurities and instabilities that in traditional salaried, unionised work the employer typically manages. Innumerable books, TED Talks, social media content, and other popular media invite us to embrace risk and live with uncertainty, but there is no getting away from the plain and simple fact that creative work is invariably precarious work. The creative

DOI: 10.4324/9781003162025-1

economy is Janus-faced, but its discourse only promotes positives. Creativity and precarity are currently two sides of the same problematic coin. We can too easily lose sight of the cultural meaning of creative work as its precarities take hold. This book accepts Raymond Williams' invitation to rediscover cultural meaning in the everyday, by asking how we might reimagine and reconstitute creative work as less precarious and more ordinary.

Creative work

Selina is a London-based poet. When we met to discuss her work, she shared with me moments from her life that inform why and how she reconciles distinctions and similarities between her work and artistic practice:

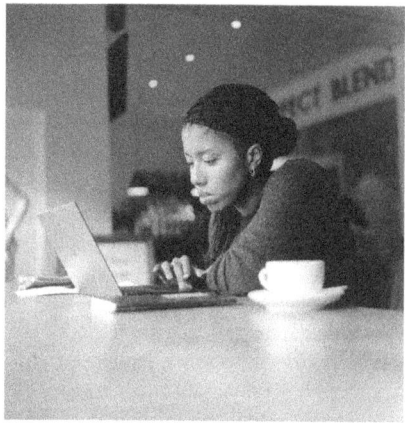

Image credit: Tim Butcher

'For better or worse, I've always seen what I do in two parts; the kind of policy research, human rights side of things and then the creative side of things. Even though there's still this divide, everything I do now is in a freelance capacity and so it's now kind of blurring in a way that it wasn't previously.'

'When I first came to London, I did internships, but it was really hard to find a job, I was in and out of work for years. This was really scarring and that precarity was awful. But I also think it encouraged me to pursue other creative avenues, because what did I have to lose?'

'Though my experiences with work have since changed, I've seen my creative work move and progress in a way that it hasn't with traditional work. Opportunities and trust in what you can achieve continue to feel very different creatively as opposed to the hierarchies of traditional institutions. I noticed this very quickly once I started working and writing at the same time.'

This vignette co-curated[1] from our discussions illustrates how Selina makes sense of becoming freelance. Through experience, Selina has found a way of working that has led to her work and practice converging. There is seemingly no external coercive force that drove Selina towards freelancing, just her experiences of precarity and her desire to do meaningful work. This way of combining work and practice into Selina's creative work is common but not the same for all artists and creatives. How Selina describes creative work is though indicative of how we internalise creative economy discourse, but it is not the only way of talking about creativity and precarity. We each experience the power within the discourse and make sense of our individual relationships with it differently. There are various ways in which we engage with the creative economy and narrate our experiences but, as will be shown, the common thread is how we individually internalise creativity and precarity to fuel our desires to do meaningful work. It is that commonly felt but individualised affective experience that will be unpacked and understood through the book.

To rethink creative work, a working definition of its current manifestations is necessary. That working definition of what constitutes creative work, based on this brief introduction, is proposed as an internalised desire to do meaningful work that stems from a will to be creative, informed by individual experiences of precarity. As mentioned, we each have our own experiences and therefore our own understandings of creativity and precarity. The chosen moniker of creative work may not sit well with everyone. You may, for example, take issue with the very notion of creativity, as Bayles and Orland (1993, p. 100, emphasis in original) vehemently do: 'Readers may wish to note that *nowhere* in [their] book does the dreaded C-word appear.' Or you might argue that precarity does not accurately represent contemporary workers' experiences, as Woodcock (2021) suggests. These words are though cornerstones of contemporary discourses of work and life. They are part of the language used to make sense of our felt experiences 'for better or worse.' As will be argued, regardless of labels, the materialities and immaterialities of pursuing an artistic practice or creative career in the current creative economy inhabit us in deeply affective ways. It is through the discourse currently available to us that we use particular language to make sense of those feelings – to give meaning to why we do creative work. However, within the discourse of creativity, there is a political power that reinforces the notion that to be creative we must experience precarity. This is a false dichotomy that produces problematic subjectivities, which this book will seek to critically understand. Why we take issue with terms like creativity and precarity is because they are empty signifiers – they have no specific referent and so are open to interpretation, appropriation and therefore subject to power (Laclau, 2014). The political and economic use of terms like creativity and precarity to perpetuate the idea of a creative economy dilutes and distorts our experiences of them. This book will therefore deconstruct the aforementioned working definition to rework it in order to give new, more tangible meaning to creative work.

This book recognises and respects the diversity of artistic practices, forms of creative work and the multitude of perspectives on what they are and are not. Each perspective stems from our individual relationship with our practice and how we constitute it and ourselves within creative economy discourse. Where some might resist the dominant discourse through critical artistic practice, others might ambivalently adopt the economic language of creativity. Regardless of how we each internalise the discourse, it is ever-present, and we use it. For independent performance artists to be commissioned or for freelance graphic designers to tender for work, for example, they must each speak the language of the creative economy to some extent, no matter how uncomfortable it may feel. My own discomfort with the discourse inspired the research which informs this book. The working definition of creative work is therefore thoroughly considered and critically deployed to problematise the political economy in which it is situated. It will be unpacked conceptually to come to terms with its materialities in a way that does not merely create new labels or recycle old ones, but moves beyond representations of what artistic practice, creativity, precarity and work are, to render the working definition obsolete, rethink those concepts and map out how we might work in new ways that refuse the current discourse, towards developing a new language of creative work. This rhizomatic approach is an attempt to put down roots that might propagate an alternative discourse – one that is less precarious and more ordinary; less economically driven and more culturally meaningful.

It should of course be noted that this is not the first text to examine this phenomenon (see e.g. Banks, 2007; Gerber, 2017; McRobbie, 2016; Beech, 2019). Neither is the creative economy the only context in which creativity is encouraged and precarity felt. Indeed, many artists and creatives take on work in other economic sectors such as hospitality or the gig economy to support themselves and their families, and to sustain their practices. Such fragmentation of individuals' working lives characterised by dependencies on typically low-wage, short-term, flexible work is increasingly common in post-Fordist societies – post-industrial societies that are no longer sustained by jobs in large-scale mass production but instead by employment that is all about communication and consumption (after Lazzarato, 2014). As will be discussed, the creative economy and its discourse emerged from the State's recognition that new more flexible forms of work were required for a growing population of current and future generations with increasingly limited access to salaried, secure jobs in traditional (i.e. Fordist) industries. So, before creative work can be reimagined, this contemporary global economic phenomenon must first be understood.

Creative economy

It would be easy but wrong to long for a 'rediscovery' of a (mythical) golden era of artistic freedom unshackled from any necessity to earn a living. There is a problematic history of romanticising artistic practice as non-economic and anti-capitalist (Beech, 2019). It sets up an unhelpful and irrelevant antagonism that over-simplistically positions the arts outside of mainstream economic activity, reinforcing the myth of the struggling artist and ignoring the lived realities of contemporary artists and creatives. As Boltanski and Chiapello (2005/2017) show, the idea of artistic freedom that has long been enacted as a rejection of petit bourgeois complicity in capitalist consumption but has, since the advent of neoliberalism in the mid-1970s, discursively transformed into a means of flexiblising post-Fordist labour. Where the aesthetic expression of free choice (through not only the making of art but '*living* the life of an artist') can be experienced as an escape from the apparent mundanities of provincial or suburban life, this idealised lifestyle has been absorbed into and overtaken by contemporary political and economic logics that promote creativity and self-determination as fundamental means for individual success. Why? Because secure and stable jobs rarely exist today.

Simply put, neoliberal promotion of global free trade via deregulation of industry and privatisation of the public sector through the 1980s and into the 1990s not only necessitated restructuring of labour markets, but it also produced a significant social decline in post-industrial regions and inner-cities (Gerosa, 2021). As the means of production relocated elsewhere in the world, social and cultural voids were created. As part of its agenda, the State's solution was to persuade us to take responsibility for filling those voids. What neoliberalism has succeeded at is liberating so many of us from the supposed mundanities of the previous Fordist mode of capitalism by preoccupying us with the consumption of not only commercial goods and services but the ideals they promote (Fleming, 2017) – the things we now consider culturally important.

Cunningly, neoliberal discourses confuse two interpretations of liberation (Boltanski and Chiapello, 2005/2017), where:

> Liberation can be understood as deliverance from a condition of oppression suffered by a people, or as emancipation from any form of determination liable to restrict the self-definition and self-fulfilment of individuals.
>
> (1095)

Where emancipation is the idea of artistic freedom, deliverance is commonly experienced as self-determination – an escape from exploitation (Boltanski and Chiapello, 2005/2017). Everyday ideals such as 'work-life balance,' or 'escape from the cubicle farm' that we consume through various communication channels conflate self-determination with artistic freedom to empower us to imagine working in evermore innovative, independent and flexible ways that offer us 'lifestyle choices.' These conflated ideals of freedom and choice that today we take for granted serve to occupy us at work more than ever.

Many aspects of contemporary labour are immaterial (Lazzarato, 2014). So many contemporary forms of work that are experienced as being creative are designed to produce the cultural content of goods and services as the means to circulate information in economies sustained by consumption (Lazzarato, 2014). And interestingly, we tend to design many of those non-material communicative work tasks ourselves, as we attempt to make them tangible in our search for meaning through work. From freelance app developers building code to tenured professors constructing knowledge, so many of us convince ourselves that we are doing creative work to give meaning to our immaterial labour. In either case, producing digital content, for example, provides ways to produce outputs for consumption – to say something along the lines of: 'I made this for this reason, and it's real, new and necessary.' We feel empowered to find creative solutions to problems that did not previously exist; we work on those solutions in our free time as well as during working hours; and we do so to emancipate ourselves from notions of mundanity and exploitation. Yet, what we are in effect doing is exploiting ourselves, calling it lifestyle choice to remain employable (Bloom, 2016; Cremin, 2010).

This is a stark sketch of creative work. Generally, we engage ambivalently in immaterial labour, working harder and harder to create opportunities to liberate ourselves from mundanity and exploitation, because the freedom such work promises is so all-consuming. Our individual sense of self has become bound up in what we do for a living more than ever before – who we are is what we do. Neoliberalism has convinced us we are individually autonomous and self-reliant enough to create our own futures (Bröckling, 2016). To be creative now is to not only create new things (i.e. goods, services and the ideals they embody) but also to creatively define our own working conditions. The discourse of creativity is entangled with that of entrepreneurialism (Bröckling, 2016). In the current post-Fordist epoch, the entrepreneurial self (Bröckling, 2016) is heralded for its individual creativity to work independently and innovatively, to contribute to contemporary culture and society but more importantly for the neoliberal project to continue to generate capital flows and economic growth. While we may be working towards individual freedom, we are not only complicit in capitalist consumption, we perpetuate it with little or no external pressure on us to do so. Arguably, the pursuit of creative freedom is the preoccupation of the new petit bourgeoisie – we are consumed by our constant striving.

There is seemingly no external force that drives us to work, just our internal desires to do something meaningful for ourselves. Metaphorically, we bring ourselves to work each day and we return home at night confronted by the realities of being so self-reliant, so independent, so precarious (after Fleming, 2017). Literally, what is increasingly common is that work and home are no longer so dichotomous, but are incidental spaces in which our entrepreneurial selves work to live and live to work – the blurred everyday spaces through which those internalised tensions play out all day and all night (after Gregg, 2011). As work is detached from traditional forms of employment and social support, it becomes increasingly insecure, uncertain, unstable and therefore precarious (Kalleberg, 2018). Maurizio Lazzarato pointedly sums up our current predicament:

> For the majority of the population, to become an economic subject ('human capital,' 'entrepreneur of the self') means no more than being compelled to manage declining wages and income, precarity, unemployment, and poverty in the same way one would manage a corporate balance sheet.
>
> (2014, p. 9)

The prevalence of precarity is directly related to our increasing self-reliance and entrepreneurialism, all of which is motivated by our desires to be creative. The creative economy imaginary is, as was suggested earlier, a powerful, pervasive, Janus-faced discourse that drives us to act in evermore individualised ways.

In particular, creative economy discourse empowers us to explore our creativity in order to fill the social and cultural void left by the implementation of the neoliberal project of the 1980s. The creative economy was originally imagined in the 1990s as a panacea for the social decline that resulted from deregulation and privatisation (Gerosa, 2021) – a thoroughly neoliberal solution to the problem of neoliberalism. The idea of a creative economy, propagated in the 1990s most notably in the UK through the political rhetoric of the incoming New Labour government, leveraged its valorisation of artistic practice to arrest both declining cultural participation and rising unemployment, by generating new forms of creative work in order to stimulate economic growth and make up for the shortfall in social support (Gerosa, 2021; O'Connor, 2021) – work ranging from participatory art to social entrepreneurship, or from architecture to advertising. The UK was not alone; the rhetorical repositioning of cultural production as mainstream economic activity was at the same time being promoted through the popular writing of the likes of Richard Florida and Charles Landry to implant ideas of 'a creative class' working in 'creative cities.' Also often referred to as the cultural industries[2] (Banks,

2007) or the creative and cultural industries (Tanghetti, Comunian and Dent, 2022), the creative economy imaginary (Gerosa, 2021) was implanted in the public consciousness globally.

Cities such as London and New York gained significant public-private investment in creative projects to regenerate inner urban areas that were labelled as being in stark decline for decades. Meanwhile, school curricula were adjusted to encourage creativity, not so that young people would aspire to become artists, but to promote the autonomy and self-reliance necessary to work in post-Fordist economies (Bishop, 2012). Into the 2000s, cities such as Portland, Oregan and Berlin became hubs for individuals working in any number of new and exciting work roles not previously defined, in repurposed workspaces designed to inspire creativity and innovation. Coworking spaces and innovation hubs took over disused inner urban spaces that may have once been occupied as squats or artist collectives, to provide flexible, connected workspaces for an increasing number of self-reliant, independent workers in search of creative careers and a certain post-industrial aesthetic (Butcher, 2016).

The eco-system of globally connected individuals in contemporary urban sites that Florida and others envisaged has come to fruition, and the creative economy feels very real indeed. In sewing that seed in our minds, so many of us can imagine ourselves as creatives with freedom to work how, when and where we wish. The imaginary is evocative, empowering and embedded in the everyday. The scope of cultural production has increased exponentially to generate work that did not previously exist – to construct the global creative economy. The ordinary notion of culture that Raymond Williams experienced in the 1950s has been overtaken. What Williams envisaged was cultural democracy through which we all equally have access to the arts and culture in our everyday lives (Cuddy-Keane, 2003; Meade and Shaw, 2007). What has materialised via the creative economy is a democratisation of cultural production by empowering so many of us to reimagine ourselves.

Creative work is therefore entrepreneurial work, whether we like it or not. Entrepreneurial archetypes are problematic but play into how the creative economy functions. The naturalisation of the entrepreneurial self takes place in every corner of society, from school education to advertising. Children are taught to be self-reliant from an early age and we are constantly reminded by the media and each other of our autonomies. For some that is enticing, for others it is daunting. The mainstay of contemporary cultural consumption is therefore to support our sense of self, to reinforce our desires to create, and distract ourselves from our precarities. A further objective of this book is therefore to question creative work's relationship with entrepreneurialism to free it from archetypal striving and self-exploitation. Its overall aim is to understand whether if at all creative work can be liberated from its economic shackles.

Chapter summary and outline of the book

This opening chapter has introduced a significant problem that underpins work and life in the creative economy – the compounding experience of feeling both creative and precarious. It is compounding, in so much as these two internalised empty signifiers are in constant dialogue with each other – the more we strive to work creatively, the more precarious we feel, so long as we continue to subscribe to current creative economy discourse.

So far, it has been argued that to remove feelings of precarity from creative work, we need to not just rethink the discourse, but to shift it from an economic one to something more culturally meaningful, something more grounded in ordinary everyday life – to free it from economic logics. However, as Richard Hoggart, another key cultural theorist suggests, we should not go in search of a sort of honest-to-goodness ordinariness from a mythical past in the hope that this inspires us to eventually do the right thing (1957/1962). There is no place for romanticism or nostalgia in repurposing creativity. It cannot be expected that ordinary everyday morality will shine through and the State, employers, and we ourselves recognise the fallacies of neoliberalism to adjust the terms and conditions of our labour in good faith. Instead, the empty signifier of creativity first needs to be filled with new meaning by demonstrating how and why it can be reimagined. That is the principal purpose of this book.

This book asks the critical question: why and how should creative work be reimagined? To answer this two-part conundrum, the book first understands the *why* by showing how we currently seek to reconcile the internalised dialectical tension between creativity and precarity. It then addresses the *how* by reconceptualising creative work and proposing an alternative approach to experiencing it that is capable of redefining why we engage in it. In other words, this book seeks to give new meaning to creative work.

Conceptually, the book examines precarious work and explores its politics and affects to show how we internalise creative economy discourse and how we might contest it (Chapters 2–3). Then, empirically it examines how our creative intentionalities can be redirected, or more precisely experienced differently to redefine why we do creative work and thus the purpose it serves in society (Chapters 4–5). Uniquely, this book identifies the potential for a radical disjuncture from the dominant discourse to not only repurpose creativity but to also contest the naturalisation of precarity in society in general (Chapters 6–7).

As the world becomes ever more unstable, uncertain and insecure, it is timely and necessary to redefine the terms and conditions of our labour, whether we consider ourselves creative or not. The COVID-19 global pandemic coupled with highly volatile geo-politics expose the shortcomings of the State's absolution of its responsibilities to sustain culture and society and the problematic power structures that dictate the discourse. As populations grow, natural resources are depleted, structural inequalities increase and the cost of living rises, we work harder and harder to be employable for less and less reward. If we accept that precarity is the norm, what meaning will there be in life? What hope will we have? Continued consumption to distract ourselves from our lived realities is not the answer. And so creative work must be redefined to free it from this ever-decreasing circle. This book therefore attempts to discover a new kind of ordinariness in creative work that can offer hope for a society in which culture is not consumed as commodities to distract ourselves from our precarities, but as something mobilised to contest the power that perpetuates precariousness. The disparities between the lifestyles we try to create for ourselves and the actual everyday realities of fending off precarity loom over too many of us.

This book seeks to show what creative work is today and how it might be reimagined for tomorrow. Its argument is supported by vignettes from interviews with artists and creatives like Selina, to elucidate concepts that underpin the book's theoretical framework and case studies. The key concepts that will be discussed are grounded in the everyday but need to be unpacked in order to rethink them, because it is their everydayness, their taken-for-grantedness that the discourse exploits. To shift the discourse, we must rethink and rewrite such concepts based on what we already know about their materialities and immaterialities. That could (but won't) be done in a way that removes those concepts from the everyday, rendering them unwieldy and leaving you asking how any of this relates to you. Instead, throughout the book, the conceptualisation of creative work will be applied to the work and lives of contemporary artists and creatives, to establish a rich picture of how lived experience informs the proposed reconceptualisation.

Notes

1 Refer to the appendix for discussion of research methods.
2 Creative economy, cultural industries, or creative and cultural industries are typically used to identify the same phenomenon. This is indicative of the discursive shifts and ambiguities as cultural, social and economic policy have changed and merged over the past 30 years (Loacker and Śliwa, 2018). This book adopts the language of the book series for consistency.

References

Banks, M. (2007) *The politics of cultural work*. Basingstoke: Palgrave Macmillan.
Bayles, D. and Orland, T. (1993) *Art and fear: Observations on the perils (and rewards) of artmaking*. Sacramento, CA: Image Continuum.
Beech, D. (2019) *Art and postcapitalism: Aesthetic labour, automation and value production*. London: Pluto Press.
Bishop, C. (2012) *Artificial Hells: Participatory Art and the Politics of Spectatorship*, London: Verso.
Bloom, P. (2016) 'Work as the contemporary limit of life: Capitalism, the death drive, and the lethal fantasy of "work – life balance"', *Organization*, 23(4), pp. 588–606. DOI: 10.1177/1350508415596604.

Boltanski, L. and Chiapello, È. (2005/2017) *The new spirit of capitalism*. Translated by Elliott, G. London: Verso.

Bröckling, U. (2016) *The entrepreneurial self: Fabricating a new type of subject*. London: Sage.

Butcher, T. (2016) 'Co-working communities: Sustainability citizenship at work', in Horne, R., Fien, J., Beza, B.B. and Nelson, A. (eds.) *Sustainability citizenship in cities: Theory and practice. Advances in urban sustainability*. Abingdon, Oxon: Routledge, pp. 93–103.

Cremin, C. (2010) 'Never employable enough: The (im)possibility of satisfying the boss's desire', *Organization*, 17(2), pp. 131–149. DOI: 10.1177/1350508409341112.

Cuddy-Keane, M. (2003) 'Defining cultural democracy: Modernism and universal individualism', *Key Words: A Journal of Cultural Materialism*, 4, pp. 56–77. Available at: www.jstor.org/stable/45367750.

Fleming, P. (2017) *The death of homo economicus: Work, death and the myth of endless accumulation*. London: Pluto Press.

Gerber, A. (2017) *The work of art: Value in creative careers*. Palo Alto, CA: Stanford University Press.

Gerosa, A. (2021) 'The hidden roots of the creative economy: A critical history of the concept along the twentieth century', *International Journal of Cultural Policy*. DOI: 10.1080/10286632.2021.1933460.

Gregg, M. (2011) *Work's intimacies*. Cambridge: Polity Press.

Hoggart, R. (1957/1962) *The uses of literacy: Aspects of working-class life with special reference to publications and entertainments*. Harmondsworth: Penguin Books.

Kalleberg, A.L. (2018) *Job insecurity and well-being in rich democracies*. Cambridge: Polity Press.

Laclau, E. (2014) *The rhetorical foundations of society*. London: Verso.

Lazzarato, M. (2014) *Signs and machines: Capitalism and the production of subjectivity*. Translated by Jordan, J.D. South Pasadena, CA: Semiotext(e).

Loacker, B. and Śliwa, M. (2018) 'Beyond bureaucracy and entrepreneurialism: Examining the multiple discursive codes informing the work, careers and subjectivities of management graduates', *Culture and Organization*, 24(5), pp. 426–450, DOI: 10.1080/14759551.2016.1167691.

McRobbie, A. (2016) *Be creative: Making a living in the new cultural industries*. Cambridge: Polity Press.

Meade, R. and Shaw, M. (2007) '[Editorial] community development and the arts: Reviving the democratic imagination', *Community Development Journal*, 42(4), pp. 413–421. https://doi.org/10.1093/cdj/bsm032.

O'Connor, J. (2021) 'The great deflation: Arts and culture after the creative industries', *Making & Breaking*, 2. Available at: https://makingandbreaking.org/article/the-great-deflation-arts-and-culture-after-the-creative-industries/ (Accessed: 2 February 2022).

Tanghetti, J., Comunian, R. and Dent, T. (2022) 'Covid-19 opened the pandora box of the creative city: Creative and cultural workers against precarity in Milan', *Cambridge Journal of Regions, Economy and Society*, rsac018. DOI: 10.1093/cjres/rsac018.

Williams, R. (1958/1989) 'Culture is ordinary', in Gable, R. (ed.) *Resources of hope*. London: Verso, pp. 3–18.

Woodcock, J. (2021) *The fight against platform capitalism: An inquiry into the global struggles of the gig economy*. London: University of Westminster Press.

2 How being creative became precarious

Work and meaning

> To talk among ourselves, about what needs to be done and how best it can be done, is so natural that when it fades away into an uneasy silence we can usually be certain that something is wrong. This is the meaning of human work . . . : an articulation of need, a definition of co-operative means, in what is felt and known to be a common condition.
>
> (Williams, 1968/2022, pp. 71–72)

As Raymond Williams describes it, any form of work can be meaningful. Work, paid or unpaid, offers us a sense of purpose in life. What access we have to work, what sort of work we do, why and how we do it inform our selfhood in relation to others. We negotiate the social order of society based, to a large extent, on who we are as workers – work informs ideas of social class and status (Williams, 1968/2022). Work is not just an everyday necessity, it is an important discursive field in which our moralities and politics play out (Komlosy, 2014/2018). As introduced in Chapter 1, contemporary creative work is bound up in complex discourses of selfhood through which we can feel both creatively empowered and precariously disempowered in the same moment.

Who we work for is a critical consideration if we are to understand the relationship between the work we do and our sense of self. In his essay on the meanings of work, Williams (1968/2022) notes how work has been abstracted into labour under the conditions of capitalism through relationships between those who offer work (i.e. capitalists) and those seeking work (i.e. workers). This is the labour market, the economic means for reducing the meaning of work into a profitable return on the investment of capital (Williams, 1968/2022). For Williams (besides Marx, Engels and other theorists of the political economy, culture and society before and after him), this is the root of the modern class system; the thing that Williams and his contemporaries such as Richard Hoggart and E.P. Thompson identified as restricting access to education and cultural participation for those bound to a life of labour. As Komlosy outlines, social and political discourses commonly position work's

DOI: 10.4324/9781003162025-2

self-actualising potentialities against notions of freeing humanity from a compulsion to work (2014/2018). Yet, these are not necessarily opposing ideals, but are discursively entangled in various ways: 'transforming the toil and burden of work into creativity and satisfaction' (Komlosy, 2014/2018, p. 44). It is this transformative potential that Williams argues for in suggesting we 'talk among ourselves' about our experiences of work. Work is central to the egalitarian concept of cultural democracy, which invites equal access to education and ordinary, everyday cultural participation. Meade and Shaw (2007) connect cultural democracy to Williams' conception of culture as being the most ordinary common. Williams' theory of cultural materialism views culture as embedded in the materialities of the everyday and a means through which to express class struggle (Eagleton and Williams, 1987/1989). He is interested in a cultural totality – the whole experience of life in a specific place and all its complexities (Hall, 1983/2016). Williams' notion of ordinariness is more complex than the nostalgia, Hoggart (1957/1962) considers it to be. Different cultural experiences and readings of experience produce contestations over meanings (Cuddy-Keane, 2003). Hence, through practical engagement with the material realities of the everyday, we can come to understand what we are free to do (Williams, 1978/1989). Significantly, cultural democracy for all can only be achieved, William's argument suggests, by reimagining work (1968/2022).

Mario Tronti notes that Karl Marx makes an important distinction between the labour process and the process of valorisation, to inform how we should consider the material relations of work (1966/2019). The labour process is not itself coercive, because the worker consumes the means of production as material for their productive activity. Whereas, in capitalism, the opposite is true – the means of production consumes the worker by giving value to (i.e. valorising), or capitalising on their labour. Within capitalism, workers are compelled to provide surplus labour and therefore to produce surplus value. 'Capital sees the labour process only as a process of valorisation; it sees labour-power only as capital' (Tronti, 1966/2019, p. 12). In other words, the worker is not exploited by their labouring per se, but by capitalists' desires to extract value from their labour. The interesting thing about contemporary creative work within neoliberal, post-Fordist capitalism is that we tend to work for ourselves (Bröckling, 2016) – we actively seek to generate surplus value from our own labour. Hence to reimagine such contemporary work as a co-operative means for cultural democracy, as Williams suggests, or to escape from (self-)exploitation and precarity as argued in Chapter 1 (after Boltanski and Chiapello, 2005/2017), the valorisation of creative work must be examined.

Work in a precarious labour market

The market is where labour value is determined by those who seek a profitable return on their investment in that labour. Dario Gentili (2021) makes a fundamental point about how the labour market operates under neoliberal capitalism:

> The discourse of the market controls conduct by means of the constant threat of 'mortal danger', eliciting that sense of vulnerability and precariousness experienced during an epidemic. This includes marginalization, poverty, unemployment – the risk of not surviving if one is not able to compete in the 'meritocracy' of the market. The entrepreneurial risk of the self-employed neoliberal individual always goes hand in hand with the precariousness of their position in the cosmos. This is a condition that entrusts the success or failure of the enterprises to the market, which shares the inscrutability of the cosmos's ends and designs.
>
> (Gentili, 2021, p. xviii; emphasis in original)

Neoliberalism is a politics of crisis (Gentili, 2021). It is an interregnum between the dying out of the old order dominated by the traditional Fordist means of mass production and the birth of a new order. Post-Fordism is therefore not a new means of production, but a way of describing the adjustments of the labour market to life and work (at least in the Global North[1]) without the relative certainties and securities of mass production. The work done now in this post-Fordist epoch is therefore not necessarily how work will be in the future. Instead, work is being reconfigured to adapt to crises discursively generated by the market. Popular contemporary tropes such as the entrepreneurial self and creative freedom are part of a discourse that is not necessarily trying to work out what the new order might look and feel like (though it is often framed as such), but one that generates apparent necessity for individual survival through current crisis. Emma Dowling notes that by attempting to fix each crisis, we do not address their causes, but displace them (2021). Following Gentili's logic, discourses of creativity and precarity therefore fill the current interstices between the past and future of work. They do not represent what the future of creative work could become. And so, this offers a glimmer of hope that the future of work need not be consumed by crises or precarity.

Such a future may though currently seem difficult to imagine. Employing Michel Foucault's concept of *dispositifs* and following Antonio Gramsci's logic of hegemony, Gentili argues that neoliberalism produces market crises to maintain its power because it creates no alternatives to its current institutional structures (2021). Neoliberalism was not conceived to construct new state apparatus but merely to dismantle the old order through industrial deregulation and public sector privatisation, so as to free itself from its responsibilities for culture and society, effectively handing them over to the market, thereby creating powerful public-private dispositifs that enable increasingly erratic market fluctuations to prompt a pervasive sense of precarity. Government is no longer the prerogative of the State but is produced by the market (Gentili, 2021).

Peter Fleming points to how neoliberal discourses operate to motivate us to work through such apparent volatility:

> Work today is simply an ideology, designed to lock in a particular class relationship and naturalise the private ownership of the means of production. It does this by falsely evoking the ruse of physiognomic necessity: if we work in order to *live*, then only a fool would argue against the need to build society around jobs.
>
> (2017, p. 143, emphasis in original)

Class-based cultural dupes like Florida's creative class (2019) or Standing's precariat (2014) circulate within the discourse to create problematic distinctions based on how we individually consume notions of working to live (through crisis). Where the creative class holds an apparently privileged position in society of being those in a range of occupations whose work involves combining knowledge and ideas or talent to solve problems or create value (Florida, 2019), the precariat is positioned as an expanding class of worker defined by its struggles for recognition (to overcome insecurity), representation (of its voice) and redistribution (of assets/resources) towards liberation from the exploitation of its labour (Standing, 2014). Such generalised dispositions create discursive distinctions between those whose work is valued by the economy and those whose is not, those who feel empowered to confront crises head on and those who don't. Yet in each category, individuals are consumed by the ideal of working to live (after Fleming, 2017). Such finite categorisations ignore the possibility that we might feel both creative *and* precarious in our work. By subscribing to such class-based tropes, we preoccupy ourselves with whether or not our work and ourselves are valuable and what possibilities we have for a better quality of life. This is the cunning of discourses of crisis.

Working to live, the creative economy, the entrepreneurial self, and other such tropes have developed over time as discursive devises to liberate us from ideas of working for others, empowering us to work for ourselves through the perpetual economic crises created by neoliberal re-ordering, such as inner city social decline in the 1980s and 1990s, the bursting of the tech bubble (or dot-com boom) of the early 2000s, the global financial crisis of 2007–8, and the COVID-19 pandemic since 2020. Hence, where economic crises are the products of dispositifs that maintain market power, meritocratic valorisation of creative work as the panacea for the failings of the state and a pathway to a better quality of life are the governmentalities that consume us.

In taking on individual responsibility for perpetually creating solutions to the problems of the market, we internalise the crises. This is central to

Foucault's theory of biopolitics (2004/2008), through which we govern ourselves via constant internal dialogue, for example, between creativity and precarity:

> As such, it is only the life of precarious workers that holds together the broken fragments of their working selves, which are often in opposition, and which push them into forced decisions, as if they were suspended between life and death.
>
> (Gentili, 2021, p. 103)

To stave off the 'deathly' sense of precarity, we seek the vitality in life that contemporary labour promises. The conflation of self-determination and artistic freedom in neoliberal discourses of work that Boltanski and Chiapello (2005/2017) unpack, is for Gentili a very specific notion of liberation: 'neoliberalism presupposes a cosmic order that produces its own peculiar form of individuality' (2021, p. 117). Gentili sees the entrepreneurial self not as seeking the freedom to offer work to others (i.e. to be a capitalist), but as seeking the unfettered freedom of the nineteenth-century flâneur to saunter through society as an observer of life (2021). Popular ideas such as the 4-hour work week (see Ferris, 2007/2011) claim to enable us to achieve such a lifestyle. Flânerie has become a thoroughly meritocratic ideal, but few (if any) of us can simply step back from work and observe life. What Gentili suggests is that we seek life outside of the class system – a bohemian quality of life in which we feel free from and beyond classification (after Gentili, 2021). Nevertheless, while the ideology of working to live circulates through culture and society, such liberation can seem achievable *but* is never quite within reach. The enigma of post-Fordist work is that we feel empowered to work harder and harder in the increasingly volatile and disempowering labour market to make more time for ourselves, not necessarily more money.

And so this peculiar individual, the flâneur is effectively a fantasy that many of us play out each day. Although we might experience discrete moments of liberation, Fleming's physiognomic necessity (2017) to work to live remains so long as we are embroiled in the crises created by the market. The idea that we are individually responsible for solving market crises generates a sense of both creativity *and* precarity that tethers us to the valorisation of our labour. So long as we seek to extract sufficient surplus value from our creativity in the hope of making time to live the life of the flâneur, we remain subjects of the labour market – the thing that maintains the class system; the very thing we are trying to escape from.

So, if the meritocratic pursuit of freedom confines us to the neoliberal hamster wheel, we should look to ways of working that dismiss notions of us being individually responsible for solving market crises and attempt to stop that wheel. Work has the potential to hold deeper cultural and social meaning than what current dispositifs would have us believe. Williams' notion of talking among ourselves about our experiences of work is perhaps at least a starting point for such a radical reimagining of the cosmic order that Gentili describes.

Community arts and cultural democracy

If the labour process itself does not subjugate workers, then the problem that this book is interested in is the valorisation of labour in the current creative economy and how that creates class-based distinctions based on what sorts of work we do. Specifically, what will be examined is how current notions of creative work came to be deemed valuable enough to become a core economic activity. To show how the value of creative work has changed over time as neoliberalism has taken hold, the case of the community arts movement of the 1970s and its contemporary equivalent, socially engaged art, are examined. In discussing the transition from community to socially engaged arts work, it will be shown how the valorisation of creativity and particular precarities became features of socially engaged arts work.

The community arts movement was a distinct phenomenon of the 1970s in the UK, emerging from the political moment of the late 1960s when worldwide student and worker uprisings including the general strike of May 1968 in France forced significant social policy reforms globally (Bishop, 2006; Jeffers, 2017a). In the UK, that moment was foreshadowed by progressive educational reforms. In the 1940s, free compulsory secondary education was introduced, and higher education was expanded in the 1960s via the creation of new universities. Access to education exposed the post-war generation of students from a broad range of backgrounds to the new field of Cultural Studies emerging through the work of radical academics such as Raymond Williams, Richard Hoggart, Stuart Hall and E.P. Thompson. In learning concepts such as cultural democracy, students were able to gain critical insights into their own relationships with culture, politics and society (Jeffers, 2017a; Jeffers and Moriarty, 2017). Consequently, a new generation of artists, some from working-class backgrounds, living in working-class communities, emerged with radical democratic ideals (Jeffers, 2017a). Democratic participation in the production and consumption of culture was central to the ethos of the community arts movement:

> The ideas that constitute cultural democracy both enable and depend upon direct participation, and take as their aim the building and sustenance of a society in which people are free to come together to produce, distribute and receive the cultures they choose.
>
> (Kelly, Lock and Merkel, 1986, pp. 39–40)

It broadly defined itself to encompass a range of arts practices, typically with disadvantaged groups to 'restore people's confidence in their ability to take an active part in the life of their community' (Rigby, 1982, p. 6). Being both rural and urban, each community had specific needs, which informed the art made. Where a rural community might run a folk festival, an urban community might produce murals; each celebrating culture through egalitarian processes of artmaking for social good rather than profit.

Hence, cultural democracy took different forms. While some arts organisations supported community activism, others used art to educate (Jeffers, 2017a). However, Jeffers and Moriarty (2017, p. 242) suggest what members of the movement had in common was their dissent; following Williams' 1961 definition of a dissenter as: 'a figure "who, though he [sic] cannot reverse the trends, keeps an alternative vision alive."' Stagflation in the 1970s UK economy dramatically increased the cost of living, with retail price inflation reaching 27 per cent in 1976 (The National Archives, n.d.). Already vulnerable communities were hit hard and community arts organisations provided support. Subsidised via the then Labour government's Social Contract policy, community arts organisations worked to 'encourage active participation by ordinary people rejecting the trend towards passive consumption in all other areas of life . . . enabling people to express local feelings and experiences' (Rigby, 1982, p. 6).

Government subsidies for community arts were largely awarded by the Arts Council of Great Britain via small grants (Jeffers, 2017a). Public patronage of the Arts favoured the performing arts over the visual arts, privileging particular practices and audiences (Baldry, 1981; Jeffers, 2017a). A 1974 Arts Council report by Harold Baldry highlighted this to influence policy change towards a more democratic distribution of subsidies (Jeffers, 2017a). The community arts movement gained a distinct funding scheme as a consequence of Baldry's report, co-funded by the Arts Council, local authorities and regional arts associations (Jeffers, 2017a). Subsidies were though minimal. A 1977 Arts Council report impressed with the outcomes achieved by community arts organisations in the scheme's first two years noted the value gained from committing less than 1 per cent of its total budget to them (Baldry, 1981; Jeffers, 2017a).

Hence, the valorisation of creative work arguably emerged in the 1970s as a re-evaluation of artistic labour in terms of who makes art, why, how and for whom. The community arts movement's egalitarian practices proved to be extremely cost-effective. In his influential 1974 report, Baldry noted that the movement was not reliant on 'organisational form, nor bricks and mortar, but the commitment and dedication of the individuals involved' (Arts Council of Great Britain, 1974, p. 7, cited by Jeffers, 2017a). Such advocacy effectively repositioned community artists as arts workers, which probably sat well with them, considering their affiliations with their local communities rather than arts institutions. Beech (2019) suggests that through the development of arts worker identities, a critical disjuncture from the dominant discourse of art as commodity was gained, and artists were now in a position to question the terms and conditions of their labour.

However, as Baldry repeatedly states in his retrospective text, *The case for the Arts* (1981), his vision for community arts was always local. Through the 1970s, he observed a vitality in locally funded projects that brought together what he calls professional and amateur artists, in which he viewed arts workers as committed individuals, not a movement (1981). Similarly, the *Community Arts Information Pack* (Rigby, 1982) frames community arts as being woven together as a tapestry of discrete yet meaningful arts encounters that brought together people from diverse backgrounds:

> Another vital change in the last few years has come in the way that community arts measures its own success. In the early stages of the movement there was often a cheerful assumption that the actual standard of the product didn't matter too much as long as plenty of people enjoyed the process. More recently, however, higher standards of product have been stressed – for the simple reason that any participant in a creative activity will get far more sense of achievement from high quality results than from mediocrity.
>
> (Rigby, 1982, p. 7)

This excerpt from a publication that sought to showcase the outcomes of various community arts projects illustrates how community arts organisations needed to adapt to significant political and economic change in the 1980s. As the Conservative government elected in 1979 instituted neoliberal policies of deregulation and privatisation, it dismantled previous social policy and local government structures. The Arts Council of Great Britain adjusted to this neoliberal move by swiftly removing community arts funding from its portfolio (Jeffers, 2017b).

The Conservative government's vision for arts institutions and organisations in the 1980s was to rebalance their public and private revenue streams (Jeffers, 2017b). Significant restructuring shifted discourses in the Arts from subsidies to investment, with the Arts Council implementing its *Making Arts Money Work Harder* partnership with local authorities that aimed to address social decline and promote urban regeneration (Jeffers, 2017b). Such discourses were influenced by populist ideas such as the New Right sociologist, Charles Murray's problematic notions of inner urban ghettos populated by a so-called underclass (Wacquant, 2004/2009). As the Conservatives were re-elected for a third term in office in 1987, Prime Minister Margaret Thatcher, infamously said in an interview:

> There is no such thing as society. There is a living tapestry of men and women and people and the beauty of that tapestry and the quality of our lives will depend upon how much each of us is prepared to take responsibility for ourselves and each of us prepared to turn round and help by our own efforts those who are unfortunate.
>
> (In Keay, 1987)

This was stated in the context of an argument for a spirit of free enterprise in school education and the government's new public-private Youth Training Scheme to the readers of the magazine, *Woman's Own*. Read in full, Thatcher's argument was for a new generation of enterprising individuals to find work for themselves and create work for others, in order to arrest rising unemployment. It was part of a patchwork of incentives that had broader economic aims to promote responsibilisation.

In the arts, the influential 1988 report *The Economic Impact of the Arts in Britain* hypothesised a notion of the arts as providing competitive advantage for a city; part of a broader agenda to increase tourism to the UK's major cities through a newly conceived heritage industry (Jeffers, 2017b). The arts were redefined as an economic rather than social good as part of a new cultural industries strategy of encouraging art institutions to enliven inner cities by expanding their operations, generating employment opportunities and addressing inner city social decline (Jeffers, 2017b). Community arts organisations were forced to adapt; not all were able to.

The rise of participatory art

With the discursive shift from subsidising art to investing in cultural production, the arts were put to work towards urban regeneration. Where arts institutions now sought private investment and developed commercial revenue streams, funding schemes for arts organisations became increasingly project-focused and outcomes-driven. The emphasis on producing high-quality results identified in the Community Arts Information Pack (Rigby, 1982) was by the late 1980s being transferred into skills needed to deliver surplus value from arts projects; with that value commonly being measured in terms of public participation in those projects.

Participatory (not community) art was being formalised as a set of practices clearly delineated from commercial art while being relatable to participants and publics (Matarasso, 2013). However, further political change and another discursive shift was necessary to naturalise participatory art (Matarasso, 2013).

Participatory art gained traction in the mid-1990s. In the UK, New Labour seized on the need to arrest social decline in its 1997 election campaign, rhetorically reframing the problem as social exclusion, with their proposed solutions aiming to provide social inclusion under its new banner of the creative economy (Bishop, 2012; Gerosa, 2021). The arts moved from the margins of Conservative government policy to the centre of economic life under New Labour (Banks, 2007). Participatory art became the flagship of its social inclusion agenda. Arts institutions attracted significant public-private investment to increase arts-based cultural participation – refurbishing and repurposing existing infrastructure, constructing new spaces, developing new offerings, and providing outreach programmes (Matarasso, 2019). The consequent restoration and enhancement of cultural heritage brought the arts and creativity to the fore of public consciousness (Bishop, 2012).

However, Bishop argues that the actual goal of increasing public participation was to promote conformity and self-sufficiency, while eliminating 'disruptive elements' of society, just as Thatcher had intended (2012; emphasis added). Importantly, creative economy policy not only sought to promote social inclusion but also to expand the definition of what counts as cultural production (Banks, 2007). The creative economy imaginary was to transform society for the new millennium, underscoring New Labour's refinement of Thatcher's vision of the UK as a post-Fordist economy with reduced welfare dependency and increased workforce flexibility (Bishop, 2012; Gerosa, 2021).

Within participatory art's broad remit, previously understated community arts practices were redefined more coherently as socially engaged art, to meet New Labour's social inclusion agenda (Bishop, 2012; Hope, 2017; Jeffers, 2017a; Matarasso, 2019). The grand challenge for socially engaged art was how to address the lack of participation of marginalised groups in mainstream culture and society – people who do not feel that the arts relate to them (Froggett *et al.*, 2011). Artist-led, non-object-based encounters, performances and collaborations using relational, dialogical and experiential ways of making art became goal-oriented and project-based to meet specific social policy goals (Belfiore, 2021).

Political change came again in 2010. The incoming Conservative government tightened the strings of the public purse in the name of austerity. Interestingly, despite sharp cuts to public spending in local government, central government investment in the arts was not significantly reduced (Matarasso, 2019). Nevertheless, cultural participation remains a pressing issue (Matarasso, 2019). This historical sketch illustrates increasingly centralised governmentalities and dispositifs implemented by shifting the discourse and popular imagination. The Arts Council, for example, remains instrumental in investment in socially engaged art through national schemes such as its *Creative People and Places* programme launched in 2013 and extended in 2018 to forge regional partnerships between cultural and social organisations (Matarasso, 2019). Matarasso (2019) sees uncanny similarities to the community arts movement's manifesto. However, through successful discursive turns has come a need for arts organisations, workers and artists to legitimise their practices (Belfiore, 2015).

Valuing socially engaged art

Socially engaged arts projects commission independent artists with particular socially engaged practices (Belfiore, 2021). Commissions are sites of investigation, reflection and action (Hope, 2017). The value of socially engaged art is in the social process of making art together, not the production of saleable object-based artworks. Participants typically have opportunities for cultural exchange – to share experiences, discuss the things that they feel marginalise them, and communicate their ideas through the art they make together. For Froggett *et al.* (2011) this is an aesthetic third, where artmaking remains as a third object or point of dialogue between its producers and consumers (i.e. between arts organisations and public audiences, and between project participants and their social contexts). Hence project vitality is essential to delivering outcomes. Coherent and robust participation philosophies and sustained long-term engagement with specific groups is therefore fundamental to gaining the value that project sponsors expect (Froggett *et al.*, 2011).

A noteworthy critique of socially engaged art is that it is depoliticised (Belfiore, 2021; Hope, 2017). Belfiore (2015) attributes this to an overarching need for socially engaged arts organisations to gain legitimacy with publicly funded project sponsors by demonstrating compliance with the public audit practices that govern them. Project governance therefore focuses investors' attention on the utility of organisational expenditure rather than meaningful care of project participants (Belfiore, 2021). This apparent neglect of participants' actual experiences by investors arguably exploits the goodwill of arts workers and commissioned artists who go the extra mile to provide space within projects for the social support that participants require, without appropriate remuneration, specialist training or support for their own wellbeing (Belfiore, 2021).

As discussed earlier, socially engaged arts projects are intimate long-term encounters, that can be confronting for participants, artists and arts workers alike. Indeed, Gerard (2020) suggests that such projects amount to the sublimation of social work into artistic forms, and Alacovska (2020) conceptualises the work of socially engaged artists as a form of care work. Hence, while arts workers and commissioned artists produce significant surplus labour to offer participants meaningful and possibly life-changing material experiences, the immaterial communication of more immediately tangible outcomes is what the market values, such as exhibitions, digital content and project reports (after Lazzarato, 2014). What is valorised is the rudimentary immaterial labour of perpetually relaying codifications and decodifications (after Lazzarato, 2014), not the abstract knowledge, general intellect and social cooperation that give cultural meaning to projects (after Banks, 2007).

Such continual generation of symbolic capital is, Lazzarato (2014) observes, a common feature of post-Fordist work and the preoccupation of the market. Such value in motion symbolises a productive market in which people are shown to be participating in art and culture (after Hardt and Negri, 2018), but fails to recognise arts workers' and artists' affective labour to produce meaningful relationships with participants that produce the vitalities required to deliver outcomes (after Federici, 2011/2020). Viewed from the cynical perspective of the market, to deliver the participation statistics, stories and evocative imagery of marginalised people engaged in making art, arts workers and artists work with participants' feelings to understand their affective lives and work towards social inclusion. From a more humanistic perspective, such affective labour is essential to enabling participants to engage in meaningful and potentially life-changing dialogue towards cultural democracy.

The perverse logic of the market locks socially engaged arts workers and artists into delivering participation by leveraging their affective desires to support participants. Immersive relationships with potentially vulnerable participants create individual obligations to see the process through no matter what the cost to them personally – their intensely affective labour is self-regulating (after Berardi, 2009). With limited recognition or remuneration tied to communicable outcomes, any work they do beyond demonstrating social inclusion is necessary but framed as their own choice. It is in several senses a Faustian bargain (after Standing, 2014) in which: their own desires for cultural democracy draw them into this work; the relationalities of the work can set up obligations to provide social and psychological support to participants; the quality of their engagement in those relationships determine project outcomes; and failure to deliver expected outcomes could jeopardise their ability to gain future project work. By immersing one's soul in socially engaged projects, arts workers and artists have the opportunity to practice creativity, but do so precariously. Referring to waitresses working for minimum wage (or less) plus tips, Emma Dowling notes:

> Workers' ability to create affective relations, are exploited in the valorisation process. But in turn, they are also manipulated and transformed for the purpose of surplus value extraction.
>
> (2007, p. 131)

As Hardt (1999) notes, affective labour is a necessary foundation for capitalist accumulation and patriarchal order. Power works through the mediation of affect (Anderson, 2014/2016).

Bern is a Brighton-based artist, educator and facilitator. Her practice is deeply affective. Bern makes 'political and socially engaged work which investigates the power of language to change perception' (O'Donoghue, n.d.). Bern engages multiple audiences over extended periods of time to construct large-scale affective bodies of work that challenge participants and audiences to critically consider injustices. When we met to discuss her work, Bern shared with me her life history involving an array of arts projects that illustrate how deeply she considers her practice and how her work affects her:

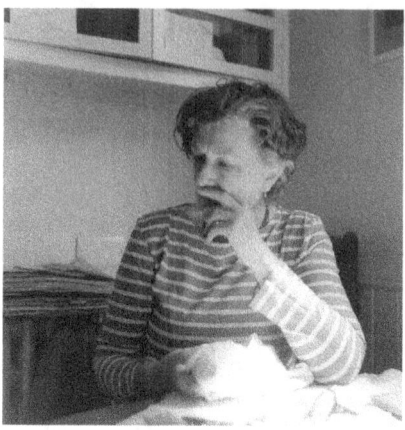

Image credit: Tim Butcher

'My work is about precarity and I live with the frustrations of being self-employed and making work which people really like to have in the world but don't always feel brave enough to stand by. . . . Being prepared to deal with something that's tricky, not shying away from it, being prepared to deal with it with people who do not want to hear about it, finding better ways of doing that, potentially dealing with their anger is quite stressful. You have to spend a lot of time making sure you're doing it for the right reasons, and you're doing it in a way that's respectful, but it's emotionally quite draining.'

'It's complicated in that a lot of artists, male and female, don't get paid properly; but a lot of women artists are paid less, and there's a complication of if you have a precarious job and if you consider it is important socially to do it, and you want to have children, it's just like massive numbers of plates spinning all the time.'

'[Socially engaged art] is one drop in an ocean of activity, but I think there definitely should be more support for this work, and it should be seen as part of society. It should definitely be seen as an integral part of a healthy society.'

In any field of creative work, it is critically important not only to name the problem of precarity, but to understand how it affects individual workers. If we are to free the soul from precarity, the workerist theorisations used here to understand the apparent entrapment of the soul in perpetual neoliberal crises must be unpacked further and an understanding of the politics of affect developed.

Note

1 The Global North is used here to define post-industrial nation states or economies. Though a global phenomenon, theories and discourses of the creative economy are still, to a large extent, produced by and circulate from the Global North.

References

Alacovska, A. (2020) 'From passion to compassion: A caring inquiry into creative work as socially engaged art', *Sociology*, 54(4), pp. 727–744. DOI: 10.1177/0038 038520904716.

Anderson, B. (2014/2016) *Encountering affect: Capacities, apparatuses, conditions.* Abingdon: Routledge.

Baldry, H. (1981) *The case for the arts.* London: Martin Secker & Warburg.

Banks, M. (2007) *The politics of cultural work.* Basingstoke: Palgrave Macmillan.

Beech, D. (2019) *Art and postcapitalism: Aesthetic labour, automation and value production.* London: Pluto Press.

Belfiore, E. (2015) ' "Impact", "value" and "bad economics": Making sense of the problem of value in the arts and humanities', *Arts & Humanities in Higher Education,* 14(1), pp. 95–110. DOI: 10.1177/1474022214531503.

Belfiore, E. (2021) 'Who cares? At what price? The hidden costs of socially engaged arts labour and the moral failure of cultural policy', *European Journal of Cultural Studies,* Online First. DOI: 10.1177/1367549420982863.

Berardi, F. (2009) *The soul at work: From alienation to autonomy.* Translated by Cadel, F. and Mecchia, G. South Pasadena, CA: Semiotext[e].

Bishop, C. (2006) 'Introduction/viewers as producers', in Bishop, C. (ed.) *Participation.* London: Whitechapel Gallery, pp. 10–17.

Bishop, C. (2012) *Artificial hells: Participatory art and the politics of spectatorship.* London: Verso.

Boltanski, L. and Chiapello, È. (2005/2017) *The New Spirit of Capitalism.* Translated by Elliott, G. London: Verso.

Bröckling, U. (2016) *The entrepreneurial self: Fabricating a new type of subject.* London: Sage.

Cuddy-Keane, M. (2003) 'Defining cultural democracy: Modernism and universal individualism', *Key Words: A Journal of Cultural Materialism,* 4, pp. 56–77. Available at: www.jstor.org/stable/45367750.

Dowling, E. (2007) 'Producing the dining experience: Measure, subjectivity and the affective worker', *Ephemera: Theory & Politics in Organization,* 7(1), pp. 117–132. https://ephemerajournal.org/contribution/producing-dining-experience-measure-subjectivity-and-affective-worker.

Dowling, E. (2021) *The care crisis: What caused it and how we can end it?* London: Verso.

Eagleton, T. and Williams, R. (1987/1989) 'The practice of possibility', in Gable, R. (ed.) *Resources of hope.* London: Verso, pp. 314–322.

Federici, S. (2011/2020) *On affective labor, in Federici, S. Revolution at point zero: Housework, reproduction, and feminist struggle*. Oakland, CA: PM Press, pp. 59–72.

Ferris, T. (2007/2011) *The 4-hour work week: Escape 9–5, live anywhere, and join the new rich*. London: Vermillion.

Fleming, P. (2017) *The death of homo economicus: Work, death and the myth of endless accumulation*. London: Pluto Press.

Florida, R. (2002/2019) *The rise of the creative class, revisited*. New York, NY: Hachette Books.

Foucault, M. (2004/2008) *The birth of biopolitics: Lectures at the Collège de France, 1978–1979*. Edited by Senellart, M., Ewald, F., Fontana, A. and Davidson, A.I. and Translated by Burchell, G. Basingstoke: Palgrave Macmillan.

Froggett, L., Little, R., Roy, A. and Whitaker, L. (2011) *New model visual arts organisations and social engagement*. Available at: http://clok.uclan.ac.uk/3024/1/WzW-NMI_Report%5B1%5D.pdf (Accessed: 2 February 2022).

Gentili, D. (2021) *The age of precarity: Endless crisis as an art of government*. London: Verso.

Gerard, N. (2020) 'Cursed creatives: Alienation, sublimation, and the plight of contemporary creative work', *Culture and Organization*, 26(5–6), pp. 388–404. DOI: 10.1080/14759551.2019.1655422.

Gerosa, A. (2021) 'The hidden roots of the creative economy: A critical history of the concept along the twentieth century', *International Journal of Cultural Policy*. DOI: 10.1080/10286632.2021.1933460.

Hall, S. (1983/2016) 'Lecture 2: Culturalism', in Daryl Slack, J. and Grossberg, L. (eds.) *Cultural studies 1983: A theoretical history*. Durham, NC: Duke University Press, pp. 25–53.

Hardt, M. (1999) 'Affective labor', *boundary 2*, 26(2), pp. 89–100.

Hardt, M. and Negri, A. (2018) *Multitude: War and democracy in the age of empire*. New York, NY: The Penguin Press.

Hoggart, R. (1957/1962) *The uses of literacy: Aspects of working-class life with special reference to publications and entertainments*. Harmondsworth: Penguin Books.

Hope, S. (2017) 'From community arts to the socially engaged art commission', in Jeffers, A. and Moriarty, G. (eds.) *Culture, democracy and the right to make art: The British community arts movement*. London: Bloomsbury Methuen Drama, pp. 203–222. DOI: 10.5040/9781474258395.ch-010.

Jeffers, A. (2017a) 'Introduction', in Jeffers, A. and Moriarty, G. (eds.) *Culture, democracy and the right to make art: The British community arts movement*. London: Bloomsbury Methuen Drama, pp. 1–32. DOI: 10.5040/9781474258395.ch-001.

Jeffers, A. (2017b) 'Then & now: Reflections on the influence of the community arts movement on contemporary community and participatory arts', in Jeffers, A. and Moriarty, G. (eds.) *Culture, democracy and the right to make art: The British community arts movement*. London: Bloomsbury Methuen Drama, pp. 133–60. DOI: 10.5040/9781474258395.ch-002.

Jeffers, A. and Moriarty, G. (2017) 'Conclusion: Opening a new space for cultural politics', in Jeffers, A. and Moriarty, G. (eds.) *Culture, democracy and the right to make art: The British community arts movement*. London: Bloomsbury Methuen Drama, pp. 1–32. DOI: 10.5040/9781474258395.ch-012.

Keay, D. (1987) 'Interview for woman's own ("no such thing as society")', *Thatcher Archive* (THCR 5/2/262): COI transcript www.margaretthatcher.org/document/106689 (Accessed: 17 February 2023).

Kelly, O., Lock, J. and Merkel, K. (1986) *Cultural democracy: The manifesto, another standard.* London: Comedian Publishing. Available at: https://dibdibdob.com/stuffandbobs/culture-and-democracy.pdf (Accessed: 17 February 2023).

Komlosy, A. (2014/2018) *Work: The last 1,000 years.* Translated by Watson, J.K. and Balhorn, L. London: Verso. eBook: ISBN 139781786634115.

Lazzarato, M. (2014) *Signs and machines: Capitalism and the production of subjectivity.* Translated by Jordan, J.D. South Pasadena, CA: Semiotext(e).

Matarasso, F. (2013) 'All in this together: The depoliticization of community art in Britain, 1970–2011', in Van Erven, E. (ed.) *Community, art, power: Essays from ICAF 2011.* Rotterdam. Available at: www.icafrotterdam.com/user_files/ICAF_2011/ICAF-community-art-power.pdf (Accessed: 2 February 2022).

Matarasso, F. (2019) *A restless art: How participation won, and why it matters.* London: Calouste Gulbenkian Foundation.

Meade, R. and Shaw, M. (2007) '[Editorial] community development and the arts: Reviving the democratic imagination', *Community Development Journal*, 42(4), pp. 413–421. https://doi.org/10.1093/cdj/bsm032.

The National Archives. (n.d.) 'World recession and the oil crisis', *The Cabinet Papers.* Available at: www.nationalarchives.gov.uk/cabinetpapers/themes/world-recession-oil-crisis.htm (Accessed: 17 February 2023).

O'Donoghue. (n.d.) *About me.* Available at: www.bernodonoghue.com/bernodmecom (accessed 20 February 2023).

Rigby, R. (1982) *Community arts information pack.* Manchester: The Shelton Trust. ISBN: 0907242014.

Standing, G. (2014) *A precariat charter: From denizens to citizens.* London: Bloomsbury.

Tronti, M. (1966/2019) *Workers and capital.* Translated by Broder, D. London: Verso.

Wacquant, L. (2004/2009) *Punishing the poor: The neoliberal government of social insecurity.* Durham, NC: Duke University Press.

William, R. (1968/2022) 'The meaning of work', in Williams, R. (Ed.) *Culture and politics: Class, writing, socialism.* London: Verso.

Williams, R. (1978/1989) 'Art: Freedom as duty', in Gable, R. (ed.) *Resources of hope.* London: Verso, pp. 88–95.

3 Affective labour, affective life, affective politics

Feeling responsible

> The transformation of humanity into a 'labor force,' a 'factor of production,' an instrument of capital, is an incessant and unending process. The condition is repugnant to the victims, whether their pay is high or low, because it violates human conditions of work; and since the workers are not destroyed as human beings but are simply utilised in inhuman ways, their critical, intelligent, conceptual faculties, no matter how deadened or diminished, always remain in some degree a threat to capital.
>
> (Braverman, 1974/1998, p. 96)

What Harry Braverman emphasises here is the human cost of valorising labour. It transforms workers into human capital. Although Braverman's analyses were of Fordist mass production, his statement remains relevant so long as value is sought from work. As shown in Chapter 2, the process of valorisation has increased in sophistication since the 1970s. So many of us now voluntarily take personal responsibility for our careers, our wellbeing and that of others (Dowling, 2021). Neoliberalism (through dispositifs such as the creative economy, care economy and gig economy) seek to maximise our self-interest by empowering us each to take our labour to the market in pursuit of a good price for it (Dowling, 2021). This individualising process of (self-) valorisation not only de-politicises our subjectivities (Belfiore, 2021; Hope, 2017), it pacifies us to minimise the threat of resistance (Mouffe, 2008/2013). This privatised, personalised responsibility for the means of production is the most common and yet taken-for-granted feature of the post-Fordist epoch (after Dowling, 2021; Fleming, 2017). We *feel* responsible. Such affective experiences and how we might mobilise them to contest creative economy discourse are what this chapter seeks to understand.

Dowling (2021) identifies an increasingly common feature of human capital, in that it is expected to always be available to the market. Specifically, Dowling refers to the phenomenon of zero-hours contracts, in which a worker is contracted to make their labour available on a particular day, but they may not be offered that work at that time (2021), as is common in the care and

DOI: 10.4324/9781003162025-3

gig economies. In the case of socially engaged art, when I interviewed Bern (see Chapter 2), she discussed how she feels that she should always be available to arts institutions and organisations at a moment's notice. A call to do a day or two's work might come at any time, sometimes just the day before. Naturalised ad hoc hiring practices in the creative economy mean that Bern and other socially engaged artists that I interviewed cannot rely on their arts practice alone to generate a sustainable income. Yet Bern also noted the feeling that they cannot turn down such opportunities for creative work. So, Bern takes other forms of paid flexible work in retail and other sectors that provide income, *and* enable her to call in at short notice to change shift if a call comes in offering her work as an artist. Flexibility is not a choice but a necessity.

Such personal responsibility to organise life and work in order to be available for opportunities that may never eventuate is in fact the opposite of the freedoms promised by flexiblisation (after Dowling, 2021). This is where the Janus-faced nature of creative work takes hold of the soul. On the one hand, artists can feel empowered to do meaningful work when a call comes offering them an opportunity to practice their creativity. On the other, a fear can set in that future opportunities might not be available to them if they don't take the one on offer at the time. Hence artists and creatives like Bern organise their lives around being ready to say yes to creative work when the call comes. This precarious situation is far more complex, recursive and deeply embodied than neoliberal logics would have us believe. It is an intense experience that plays out moment-to-moment, day-after-day in the everyday lives of artists and creatives, characterised by feelings of uncertainty, insecurity and instability. Where creative work is fundamental to one's being, the inhumanity of flexiblisation exploits individual desires to do meaningful work and produces deeply felt precarities.

So, when opportunities to do creative work arise, there is little choice but to take them. Feeling responsible and making ourselves available are cunningly hegemonic forms of self-control that preoccupy us, neutralising any possibility that we might resist the market and say no to paid creative work (Mouffe, 2008/2013). Chantal Mouffe (2008/2013) provides valuable insights into how this hegemony – the dominant ideology's manipulation of our values and belief, feeling and desires – operates and how we might reimagine our relationships with it.

Hegemonies

Crucial to our analysis, Chantal Mouffe develops Boltanski and Chiapello's (2005/2017) argument that neoliberal logics have manipulated and confused our notions of freedom:

> The aesthetic strategies of the counter-culture: the search for authenticity, the ideal of self-management, the anti-hierarchical exigency, are now used to promote the conditions required by the current mode of capitalist regulation'
> (Mouffe, 2008/2013, p. 211)

Being autonomously flexible and available have been naturalised as ideal identity constructs (after Mouffe, 2008/2013), juxtaposed against the alienation and mundanities of what we typically associate with other forms of labour – I may feel precarious, but at least I'm being creative. As indicated earlier, we learn how to creatively juggle our lives and work from an early age and are reminded every day – it is embedded in school curricula, embodied on social media, extolled by those we look to for guidance and expected of us by the market. This hegemony is so pervasive that it feels like it is the only way to be. We might try to resist the precarity we perceive to be inherent in our creative lives and work, but it feels like we are only pushing back against ourselves. It is our 'choice' to live and work as we do; it's 'no one else's fault but our own.' So we 'keep calm and carry on.'

Antonio Gramsci (c.1933/1986) notes that we might feel deceived by our choices because our thoughts and actions are not always aligned. For example, we might think creative work emancipates us, but 'being the best version of our selves' can be anxiety-inducing. However, Gramsci points out that attempting to analyse this problem individually or even at a social group level does not help us to question the hegemony over our thoughts and actions – the invisible force that produces the cultural lens through which we experience this apparent self-deception (c.1933/1986). What Gramsci shows us is that we all feel these things to some extent, and so need to appreciate why that is:

> Critical understanding of the self takes place therefore through a struggle of political 'hegemonies' and of opposing direction, first in the ethical field and then in that of politics proper, in order to arrive at the working out at a higher level of one's own conception of reality.
>
> (c. 1933/1986, p. 21)

For Gramsci, we must become individually conscious of the ideals we take for granted and treat them as common sense to see how our conceptions of our realities are 'affirmed in words' and 'displayed in effective action' (c. 1933/1986, p. 19). Mouffe (2013) understands the problem of hegemony identified by Gramsci as a discursive process of sedimentation through which the political origins of manifold practices (e.g. the creative economy) are erased and become naturalised. Through significations in the discourse (e.g. creativity equals freedom from mundanity), new needs and desires are mobilised (e.g. to be creative I need to buy myself the latest smartphone), which enables capitalism to reproduce itself (Mouffe, 2013). We are so consumed by the discourse we fail to see alternatives to the current hegemony.

The importance of Gramsci's approach is that it enables us to see that confronting the dominant hegemony is not solely the domain of traditional political institutions (Mouffe, 2013). We can take it upon ourselves to contest our subjectivities if we are sufficiently aware of the politics that inform them and understand how to do so, with cultural and artistic practices playing a central role (Mouffe, 2013). Cultural production constitutes and maintains the symbolic order of the everyday, and so art and culture can also unsettle that order (Mouffe, 2013). How we seek to unsettle and contest hegemony will influence the outcomes of our actions. Chantal Mouffe's most significant contribution is an understanding of how to participate directly in the political in ways conducive to collectively constructing alternatives to how we currently understand politics (2013).

Mouffe claims that democratic politics cannot be understood without acknowledging that the political field is driven by passions (2013). However, previous conceptualisations of the political utilise rationalist, individualistic frameworks to understand pluralistic social relations in democratic politics. Those conventional approaches assume that while there are many different perspectives and values in society (i.e. pluralism), they are fundamentally antagonistic, and through reasoned political debate differences between 'us and them' set up by this assumption will be negated through power struggles towards the goal of consensus (Mouffe, 2013; Van Buren *et al.*, 2021). However, passions, desires and affects cannot be reasoned with and are therefore not accounted for in orthodox liberal political theory (Mouffe, 2013). Rational consensus between individuals merely operates within the current hegemony because it cannot see beyond it.

Mouffe's approach to hegemony is not to view political relations as antagonistic struggles between enemies, but agonistic struggles between adversaries (Mouffe, 2013; Van Buren *et al.*, 2021). By reimagining the power struggle, Mouffe reframes political opponents as sharing common allegiances to the democratic principles of liberty and equality, while acknowledging their different interpretations (Mouffe, 2013). The goal is not to reach consensus but dissensus. Importantly, dissensus here is not only understood just as a politics of disturbance, but also as the establishment of interconnected and equivalent democratic demands that co-create an alternative hegemony (Mouffe, 2013). If we consider Gentili's contention in Chapter 2 that neoliberalism does not offer an alternative to organised capitalism (2021), post-Fordism might be thought of as a form of stasis through which neoliberal political antagonisms play out around particular crises but do not threaten the power of the market. Consensus, Mouffe (2008/2013) argues, only operates within the current hegemony. Whereas agonistic politics contest that hegemony and signify possibilities for a new one: 'It is not enough to unsettle the dominant procedures and to disrupt the existing arrangements in order to radicalize democracy' (2013, p. 32).

Hence, so long as we continue to experience creative work as a source of individual freedom, we remain bound up in crises, and fail to see life and work unbound from the market. However, Mouffe (2013) argues that creative work, or at least cultural and artistic practices can play a critical role in contesting current situations and defining alternative futures. Mouffe (2013) discusses Alfredo Jaar's artistic practice as a form of intervention that unsettles common sense by posing simple questions that trigger reflections and arouse discontent. Hence, where cultural production constitutes and maintains symbolic order in neoliberal society, it therefore also holds significant potential to unsettle it and signpost a new hegemony. This may well be why the arts have been progressively defunded (O'Connor, 2021) and depoliticised (Belfiore, 2021). So, how do we create possibilities for dissensus under these conditions?

What is affect?

A key challenge that this book seeks to address is how to connect our individual feelings of creativity and precarity to the political. Where Mouffe (2013) identifies that affects and passions are crucial in politics, she suggests a need to find ways to collectively mobilise them towards democratic designs, but does not specify how, other than arguing that the answer might be found in artistic practices such as Alfredo Jaar's. So, here we must develop an understanding of how we process affect individually and mobilise it collectively. Furthermore, to realise the potentialities of affect agonistically rather than antagonistically, it is arguable that we need to understand how to convert affective experiences (e.g. fear, anxiety, precarity) into intentionally counter-hegemonic acts. This is the tricky bit, because affects are pre-conscious experiences (Massumi, 2002). Not everyone has a vocabulary for everyday affective experiences. What might be a shame-filled embodied response to not being awarded a commission could manifest as pre-conscious anger directed to the commissioning organisation, for example, potentially causing an argument through which each human party seeks to rationalise the situation and reach a consensus about 'whose fault it was.' We feel threatened, and so we too often react to what is happening in the moment antagonistically. However, that doesn't necessarily alter how we will react the next time we experience what we feel to be rejection – we will still see the commissioning organisation as our enemy.

Agonism arguably requires a more attuned response; one through which we understand why we react in certain ways to particular situations, and learn how not to react individually but develop a collective response that leads to changes in the material conditions of such situations (after Massumi, 2002). What are at stake here are the social relations of the political – how we might develop meaningful collective action from shared affective experiences of creativity and precarity.

Mouffe (2013) refers to Sigmund Freud's observations of groups being 'held together by a power of some kind' (Freud, in Mouffe, 2013, p. 69) to suggest that potentialities lie in the collective identity of *we* that results from passionate affective investment. Contemporary theories of affect can assist us in understanding such potentialities by appreciating the processes through which pre-conscious bodily sensations are collectively experienced (Anderson, 2014/2016).

Understood as a dynamic process of embodied intensities, affect is both an organised and mediated bodily capacity and a collective condition that stems from particular material conditions (Anderson, 2014/2016; Massumi, 2002; Kosofsky Sedgwick, 2003). In any given moment a bodily response to a situation might result from multiple affects (e.g. fear, anxiety and precarity) triggered by an encounter in the present that reminds our pre-conscious bodies of experiences in the past, between our own subjectivities and those of others, and/or through material relations with objects. Affects are imbricated (Anderson, 2014/2016) – overlapping layers of pre-conscious sensations situated in the present moment and in dialogue with memories of the past (Brown and Reavey, 2015). Everything that affects us materially presupposes a range of possibilities; and every possibility presupposes a range of affects (Massumi, 2002). Our bodies are in continual dialogue with the material world, affects are always relational, always building on each other – they are what give our bodies intensity. The body has the capacity to affect and be affected, which fills it with potential (Anderson, 2014/2016).

In Baruch de Spinoza's philosophy, affect is not just a reaction but the power to act (Negri, 1999). Negri (1999) suggests that this affective power is at once singular and universal. Affects are universal in the sense that they construct commonality of desire and feeling among subjects, while consequent actions are singular in that they cannot be contained and have infinite possibilities (Negri, 1999). We cannot necessarily anticipate how we will feel in a given moment, nor what sensations we will experience, nor the actions we will take. Past experience may give us an indication, but each encounter is situational, with unique combinations of materialities and relationalities. Hence, Massumi (2002) adopts Deleuze and Guattari's theory of the virtual to show how we experience the material world as both real and in abstract. For example, we may repeatedly take the bus to work each day (the reality of going to work), but each journey differs because it is (virtually) constituted by and constitutive of multiplicities. Those multiplicities create abstractions in each journey that cannot be predetermined, nor made sense of because they happen too quickly to process cognitively but open up new potentialities as bodies respond to enfolding situations. This intense, multi-layered pre-conscious experience is virtual, not actual (Massumi, 2002). 'The body is as immediately abstract as it is concrete; its activity and expressivity extend, as on their underside, into an incorporeal, yet perfectly real, dimension of pressing potential' (Massumi, 1995). By experiencing the intensities and newness of each encounter, we might therefore reimagine both the journey and the destination. There is potential in the intensities of what can be (virtual/abstract), but not in the mundanities of what is (real) (Massumi, 2002).

Affective possibilities

So, potential for new possibilities lies in the body. That potential could participate agonistically in the political as Mouffe (2013) proposes. It could also be directed towards the market – it commonly is. Brian Massumi suggests:

> Affect is always conditioned. Its expression, as it comes to be enacted, is always selective. Every situation of encounter imposes constraints on the selection of potential that will eventuate. The expression of affect, far from being anything goes, is an expression of necessity. It is just that it is always also an expression of the necessity of invention: an ongoing validation of the rule of variation: that the world is restless at heart and never sits still. An inventive variation takes constraints as enabling. There would be no creativity of dance without the constraint of gravity. Affect assumes necessity, in the strong sense of taking it on. It takes it on in such a way as to extract from it a surplus-value of creativity.
>
> (2015, p. 208)

Hence, the material conditions through which we experience everyday life and work determine how we utilise our potentialities. If we experience the world as a marketplace in which to trade our creative potential, then we invent ways to capitalise on the possibilities we can produce. With the dominant ideology being market-oriented, that is the most likely outcome. The restless necessity of invention that Massumi describes is precisely what the neoliberal labour market has learned to harness. The abstract intensities of feeling individually empowered to be autonomously creative are what are valorised, yet contingent on lived realities of precarity. As Cameron (2019) argues, affected labour combines the uncontrollable challenges of desiring and feeling to produce a fragility of feeling in the moment. In any given moment, the virtual experience of creative work promises an abstract notion of emancipation through aesthetic expression of free choice (after Boltanski and Chiapello, 2005/2017) while our bodies toil through the realities of precarious working conditions.

From every theoretical perspective discussed, the common thread is that the fruits of our labour are merely the creation of new ways to cope with precarity. Precarious subjectivities are the norm in a market in which we continually invent new ways to realise our creative potential. Massumi's (2015, p. 208) 'ongoing validation of the rule of variation' – the difference between the ideal and the actual – speaks to Karl Marx's theorisation of capital as value in motion, through which its circulation and accumulation is maintained by our drive to create commodities that seemingly fulfil our wants, needs and desires (Harvey, 2020). The more we create, the more bound to capital flows we become. Where capital is the process, value is a social relation that is the invisible thread that takes on different material forms (Harvey, 2020). We put our heart and soul into our work, which in turn produces a fragility we must learn to cope with. Coping and self-care have been naturalised. 'Self-care obfuscates the structural causes of societal problems: if you're not coping, it's your fault' (Dowling, 2021, p. 185). Our affective desires and potentialities are de-territorialised by the circulation of capital to the point where our principal social relation is with the market (Lazzarato, 2014), commodifying our relations with each other and the world, and blurring our political relations. For Lazzarato (2014) we are not just individualised, but divided. For Sigler, 'work is one of today's essential techniques of power, which does not impose precariousness on the body merely retrospectively but controls whether and where it manifests itself – and where it does not' (2017, p. 22).

This outlook may seem bleak, but where Chantal Mouffe (2013) sees affect as a source of agonistic politics and Brian Massumi (2002) finds manifold potential for newness in the intensities of affect, Antonio Negri argues more directly that the power of affect is unlimited and only constrained by (capitalist) obstacles to its expansion: 'labor finds its value in affect, if affect is defined as the "power to act"' (1999, p. 79). Hence, Negri (1999) extends Spinoza's notion of affect as a power to act, to find a dynamism that could elude the obstacles of capitalist valorisation. Negri argues that an ontological shift is necessary to reimagine the value of affect as something irreducible to the measurement of individual labour, and something collectively transformative, enriching and expansive (1999). Similarly, Sigler (2017) suggests the need for a new bodily ontology, noting that the body is intrinsically precarious and our relationship with work can either compound or alleviate the felt experience. So, in order to dissociate creativity from precarity, we must disavow our relationship with labour by re-evaluating our affective potentialities to redirect our creative possibilities. Creative work need not necessarily be creative labour if we can agonistically redirect our affective intensities away from the market and towards the political (after Mouffe, 2013; Massumi, 2002).

The production and practice of possibilities

Richard is a London-based performance artist. In his own words:

'Richard DeDomenici is an artist of complicated European descent who specialises in backward solutions for a progressive future. Richard's urban-absurdist interventions strive to create the kind of uncertainty that leads to possibility. DeDomenici is the inventor of the Carry-Ok wearable karaoke system, crochéted crypto-currency Knitcoin, international office chair competition The Swivelympics, and pandemic singing competition The Coronavision Song Contest. Richard has performed in over 30 countries, most recently at the Digital Wild International Biennale For Art & Technology in Trondheim, Norway.'
(Unpublished email communication, 2023).

In arranging to meet Richard for the first time, he invited me to one of a number of interventions he was leading at the time. I chose beach karaoke on the banks of the River Thames, where through active participation (including singing in public), I learned that while we (and anyone) on the shoreline were free to sing and dance in this public space, the many inquisitive passers-by on the privately owned parts of the Southbank boardwalk above had fewer freedoms. 'The Thames foreshore is London's greatest temporary autonomous zone. It's one of the few remaining places in London where you can sing outdoors karaoke without being asked to stop' (DeDomenici, 2020).

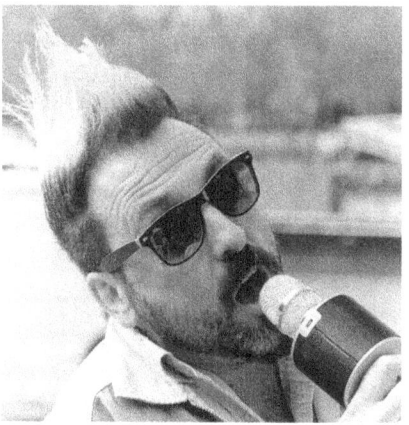

Image credit: Tim Butcher

'Years ago I read this quote by Buckminster Fuller; on his gravestone, it says "Call me trimtab." . . . A trimtab is a little rudder on the back of a ship that is very small and thin, but because of its positioning on the boat, a tiny little movement can cause a massive change in the direction of the boat.'

'It's about with temporary, small, ephemeral acts, trying to permanently change the way people look at the world, and have more critical scrutiny, and ask more questions about what they're seeing – that's my goal – but with the least amount of effort, or the least amount of input. So it's a lofty goal, and it's very hard to judge if it's working or not. You can't hand out feedback forms when you're working in the street. So there's an element of magical thinking to

> it. . . . Sometimes you just see it in people's facial expressions, even if only for a second.'
>
> 'Laughter is really good, because if you can make somebody laugh then you've broken down their natural defences and they're much more willing to engage with the underlying motive, method or meaning of the work.'

Richard's practice resonates with Mouffe's agonistic politics of dissensus (2013) and Massumi's intensities of affect (2002). When, at our first meeting, we were asked by passers-by what we were doing, Richard jovially pointed to the convivialities of beach karaoke without putting them off with a treatise about the politics of space. Meanwhile, the affective intensities I felt from performing in public in a way I'd not done before were liberating. Beach karaoke is performance art developed by Richard, uncannily using familiar practices in a space we wouldn't associate it with, which invites inquiry. As Richard suggests, it is difficult to measure its value. His practice circumnavigates obstacles of capitalism in transformative, enriching and expansive ways (after Negri, 1999). The notion of the artist as a metaphorical trimtab speaks to the role that Mouffe suggests, not necessarily steering the ship but adjusting its course as required. Mouffe is not demanding that artists lead change but that instead they invite the critical consciousness that Gramsci proposes, to encourage direct participation in political social relations that question the current hegemony and imagine alternatives.

With this understanding of how such an affective process invites direct participation, the question becomes how to build and sustain political momentum through affective social relations. As Lordon (2015/2022, p. 116) suggests: 'Human individuals do not form political groupings through some rational, contractualist process of deliberation: it is affects which hold them together, and it is worth repeating that these affects are the vehicle for ideas, values and a common symbolic realm.' What are necessary to form and hold together a counter-hegemonic movement are sustained affective intensities. The vehicle for anti-precarity ideas and values must therefore surely be a commonly felt experience of precarious work so overwhelming and all-consuming that dissensus en masse is produced. To be effective, such commonly felt experiences arguably need to be translated into conscious ordinary everyday acts.

For Raymond Williams, a common structure of feeling is rooted in fundamental values of class struggle (Blackburn, 1988; Williams, 1975/1989). The affective intensities that motivate his sociology and mobilise his activism stem from a frustration with the ignorance of those in power to ordinary culture

(Eagleton and Williams, 1987/1989; Hall, 1983/2016). Williams' theory of cultural materialism views culture as a means through which to express class struggle (Eagleton and Williams, 1987/1989). As introduced earlier, he seeks to make conscious the specificities and complexities of the everyday (after Hall, 1983/2016). 'Consciousness is no longer the mere product of social being but is at once a condition of its practical existence and, further, one of its central productive forces' (Williams, 1980/2020, p. 287). Hence, Williams finds a need to extend education to practical engagement with cultural materialities such as work to invoke a critical consciousness that facilitates direct participation in the political (1958/1989).

Williams understands direct participation as an extended dialogical process of context-specific collective acts of learning (see Williams, 1961; 1980/2020). The political is a continuous process of specific and changing relationships with culture that offers hope for what he calls cultural revolution (Williams, 1980/2020). Hence, Williams' approach is counter-hegemonic insofar as he sees ordinary everyday actions as holding potential for 'the production and the practice of possibility' (Williams, 1980/2020, p. 305; after Bahro, 1977). Significantly, Hall notes the influence of Gramsci's work on Williams after it was first translated into English in the 1970s (1983/2016).

Perhaps most importantly, within Williams' notions of culture as democratic, popular and materialist and his own academic activist practice is a pedagogical thread (Blackburn, 1988; Hall, 1983/2016). What Williams shows us is that we can develop a critical consciousness through situated, practical engagement with ordinary culture. Conceived of as perpetual learning encounters, the materialities of the body combine with everyday cultural materialities to build a structure of feeling that is in turn regenerative of culture itself. What might be interpreted as an affective momentum builds towards remaking culture from a political attunement to everyday cultural encounters with the things that signify or embody the hegemony. Depending on how we make use of our affective intensities, this generative process can either shape culture to conform to current norms or be mobilised to contest them. Williams obviously advocates the latter.

Continual dialogue through a learning process is therefore generative of the shared affective intensities necessary for the collective production and practice of possibility. For example, Jean Lave (2019) cites Paul Willis' 1977 *Learning to Labour* thesis as demonstrative of how practice is a condition of possibility for engagement in cultural production of the everyday, where Willis' working-class lads learned together how to co-produce and contest their class-based identities through practical learning in classroom situations. Such ordinary cultural encounters are not merely rites of passage, but situations through which we learn about our place in the world, how we feel about that and what we might do about it. So, we must find ways to learn together how to reimagine creative work.

References

Anderson, B. (2014/2016) *Encountering affect: Capacities, apparatuses, conditions.* Abingdon: Routledge.

Bahro, R. (1977) 'The alternative in Eastern Europe', *The New Left Review*, 106. Avaiable at: https://newleftreview.org/issues/i106/articles/rudolf-bahro-the-alternative-in-eastern-europe (Accessed: 24 May 2023).

Belfiore, E. (2021) 'Who cares? At what price? The hidden costs of socially engaged arts labour and the moral failure of cultural policy', *European Journal of Cultural Studies*, Online First. DOI: 10.1177/1367549420982863.

Blackburn, R. (1988) 'Raymond Williams and the politics of the new left', *The New Left Review*, 168. Available at: https://newleftreview.org/issues/i168/articles/robin-blackburn-raymond-williams-and-the-politics-of-a-new-left (Accessed: 30 November 2022).

Boltanski, L. and Chiapello, È. (2005/2017) *The new spirit of capitalism.* Translated by Elliott, G. London: Verso.

Braverman, H. (1974/1998) *Labor and monopoly capital: The degradation of work in the twentieth century, 25th anniversary edition.* New York, NY: Monthly Review Press.

Brown, S. and Reavey, P. (2015) *Vital memory and affect: Living with a difficult past.* Hove: Routledge.

Cameron, A. (2019) 'Reconfiguring affected labor as a site of resistance', *Capacious: Journal for Emerging Affect Inquiry*, 1(4), pp. 80–92. https://doi.org/10.22387/CAP2019.26.

DeDomenici, R. (2020) *Richard DeDomenici: Predictive texts, hope, courage BAC.* Available at: https://dedomenici.com/predictivetexts (Accessed: 15 March 2023).

Dowling, E. (2021) *The care crisis: What caused it and how we can end it?* London: Verso.

Eagleton, T. and Williams, R. (1987/1989) 'The practice of possibility', in Gable, R. (ed.) *Resources of hope.* London: Verso, pp. 314–322.

Fleming, P. (2017) *The death of homo economicus: Work, death and the myth of endless accumulation.* London: Pluto Press.

Gentili, D. (2021) *The age of precarity: Endless crisis as an art of government.* London: Verso.

Gramsci, A. (c.1933/1986) 'Prison notebooks', in Donald, J. and Hall, S. (eds.) *Politics and ideology.* Milton Keynes: Open University Press.

Hall, S. (1983/2016) 'Lecture 2: Culturalism', in Daryl Slack, J. and Grossberg, L. (eds.) *cultural studies 1983: A theoretical history.* Durham, NC: Duke University Press, pp. 25–53.

Harvey, D. (2020) 'Value in motion', *The New Left Review*, 126, November–December. Available at: https://newleftreview.org/issues/ii126/articles/david-harvey-value-in-motion (Accessed 17 February 2023).

Hope, S. (2017) 'From community arts to the socially engaged art commission', in Jeffers, A. and Moriarty, G. (eds.) *Culture, democracy and the right to make art: The British community arts movement.* London: Bloomsbury Methuen Drama, pp 203–222. DOI: 10.5040/9781474258395.ch-010.

Kosofsky Sedgewick, E. (2003) *Touching feeling: Affect, pedagogy, performativity*. Durham, NC: Duke University Press.

Lave, J. (2019) *Learning and everyday life: Access, participation, and changing practice*. Cambridge: Cambridge University Press.

Lazzarato, M. (2014) *Signs and machines: Capitalism and the production of subjectivity*. Translated by Jordan, J.D. South Pasadena, CA: Semiotext(e).

Lordon, F. (2015/2022) *Imperium: Structures and affects of political bodies*. Translated by Bliss, A. London: Verso.

Massumi, B. (1995) 'The autonomy of affect', *Cultural Critique, No. 31, The Politics of Systems and Environments, Part II*, Autumn, pp. 83–109. https://doi.org/ 10.2307/1354446.

Massumi, B. (2002) *Parables for the virtual: Movement, affect, sensation*. Durham, NC: Duke University Press.

Massumi, B. (2015) *Politics of affect*. Cambridge: Polity Press.

Mouffe, C. (2008/2013) 'Cultural workers as organic intellectuals', in Mouffe, C. (ed.) *Hegemony, radical democracy and the politics*. Abingdon: Routledge, pp. 207–215.

Mouffe, C. (2013) *Agonistics: Thinking the world politically*. London: Verso. eBook: eISBN 9781781682357.

Negri, A. (1999) 'Value and affect, (trans. Hardt, M.)', *boundary 2*, 26(2), pp. 77–88.

O'Connor, J. (2021) 'The great deflation: Arts and culture after the creative industries', *Making & Breaking*, 2. Available at: https://makingandbreaking.org/article/the-great-deflation-arts-and-culture-after-the-creative-industries/ (Accessed: 2 February 2022).

Sigler, F. (2017) 'Introduction: All that matters is work', in Sigler, F. (ed.) *Work, Documents of Contemporary Art series*. London: Whitechapel Gallery, pp. 14–25.

Unpublished email communication. (2023) 'An unpublished email exchange between the author and Richard DeDomenici', (Accessed: 15 March 2023).

Van Buren, H.J., Greenwood, M., Donaghey, J. and Reinecke, J. (2021) 'Agonising over industrial relations: Bringing agonism and dissensus to the pluralist frames of reference', *Journal of Industrial Relations*, 63(2), pp. 177–203. DOI: 10.1177/0022185620962536.

Williams, R. (1958/1989) 'Culture is ordinary', in Gable, R. (ed.) *Resources of hope*. London: Verso, pp. 3–18.

Williams, R. (1961) *The long revolution*. London: Pelican Books.

Williams, R. (1975/1989) 'You're a Marxist aren't you?' in Gable, R. (ed.) *Resources of hope*. London: Verso, pp. 65–76.

Williams, R. (1980/2020) 'Beyond actually existing socialism', in Williams, R. (ed.) *Culture and materialism*. London: Verso, pp. 282–305.

4   Collaborative learning

Making space for creative work

Today's artist-bricoleur is a compulsive inventor creating a new cultural syntax out of the debris of the already-given. Quotidian, often household items and common materials such as vacuum cleaners, trash bags, hot dog stands and duct tape are re-tooled, repaired, and re-invented.

(Sperone Wastewater, n.d.)

This is a quote from the American Bricolage exhibition catalogue of artwork shown at Sperone Westwater in New York City, 2000. The artist Tom Sachs co-curated the exhibition and showed his own work alongside contemporaries who make art from everyday objects. What is relevant to this chapter is the notion of bricolage as the production and practice of creating a new cultural syntax. Drawing on Jacques Derrida's critique of Lévi-Stauss' structuralist conception of the bricoleur as engineer, Benterrak and colleagues define bricolage as 'the activity of roaming in the ruins of culture, picking up useful bits and pieces to keep things going or even make them function better' (1984/1996, p. 168). For Derrida (1970/2014), bricolage is a phenomenon with materialities that defy fixed notions of culture because they are always adaptable.

Sachs' studio practices and aesthetic are well documented. Short films such as Ten Bullets (Sachs, 2010) give an indication of the ritualistic work ethic and the understanding of tools and materials that studio staff are expected to learn – the underlying ethos of which Sachs attributes to his time working as a janitor. Images of open workspaces with specific, well-ordered workstations where materials are colour coded to be easily identifiable can be seen in the film, Color (Sachs, 2011), everyday materials such as plywood predominate in Love Letter to Plywood (Sachs, 2012) and practices like knolling[1] have been adopted and developed. They illustrate an aesthetic more akin to a factory than conventional conceptions of artists' studios. It is an aesthetic I see mirrored in the materialities of coworking, where clearly communicated shared rituals are

DOI: 10.4324/9781003162025-4

important to maintain order and set boundaries in open spaces shared by various individuals working on their own distinct projects. And it is an aesthetic replicated and built on by the likes of Casey and Van Neistat (friends of Sachs and former studio employees) and consumed by their millions of YouTube subscribers. It is a contemporary interpretation of an age-old sensibility that communicates creativity as hard but rewarding work – a particular expression of creativity that can offer insight into contemporary interpretations of what work is and its possibilities.

'Increasingly, uncertain social and economic conditions require us to become entrepreneurially proficient, mobile and agential' (Butcher, 2018, p. 327). Casey Neistat embodies this intensely, showing millions of aspirational subscribers to his YouTube channel what a successful creative career can look like today. While he is the protagonist of his vlogs, he is constantly collaborating. Neistat runs a shared workspace: Studio 368 in New York City, with the mission 'to help creative people achieve their goals, connect with each other, collaborate and grow' (Studio 368, n.d.). Such shared workspaces, also called coworking spaces, are sites where we can come together to learn how to navigate the individualised world of work (Butcher, 2018).

Possibly the most popular academic interpretation of coworking is Spinuzzi's notion of 'working alone together' in what he calls the unoffice, which brings together elements of different types of workspaces, to enable experimentation with ways of organising work (2012). My own research extends this to show how this is made possible through specific collaborative learning practices to work through uncertainty and develop the knowledge and work ethic necessary to create individual opportunities. As Tom Sachs is often quoted as saying: 'the reward for [good] work is more work' (van de Walle, n.d.).

Although I have never heard a coworker reference Tom Sachs directly, the coworking spaces I have experienced embody both a do-it-yourself (DIY) aesthetic and a purposeful yet playful bricolage to develop the everyday rituals and routines that enable individuals to not only work alongside each other but also learn how to collaborate (Butcher, 2018). Shared practices of coworking are arguably bricolage in the way that Sachs understands and communicates it, through which coworkers purposefully seek to create collective possibilities to do good work that is generative of individual opportunities for more work.

This point is crucial to the overall argument of the book in that it lends contemporary aesthetics and materialities to Raymond Williams' vision of the production and practice of possibilities. Where Williams used his writing, television and political rallies to communicate his ideas, coworking spaces and other collaborative spaces are arguably where seemingly mundane work practices might be reimagined and reorganised to generate affective potentialities. Coworkers are typically freelancers, run start-ups or work independently (Waters-Lynch *et al.*, 2016). Many do work that didn't exist before post-Fordism, the creative economy or digital communications, and so define themselves as creatives. Hence, through the case of coworking we will explore how creative workers learn to engage collectively in the production and practice of possibilities.

Learning to cowork

Between 2012 and 2014, I coworked regularly in Melbourne, and occasionally in Sydney and London. It was a time of experimentation, when coworking space providers were learning what worked and what didn't, as members figured out how to work alone together (after Spinuzzi, 2012). Most spaces I encountered had a DIY aesthetic, housed in previously neglected post-industrial spaces hidden in plain sight in the heart of cities, and renovated on shoestring budgets. Members with diverse interests and motivations felt empowered to utilise those spaces in unorthodox ways. Materials such as plywood and coaster wheels ensured desks, chairs and whiteboards were durable, modular and moveable. Spaces could be frequently and easily reconfigured from shared desk arrangements to create meeting, event and social spaces; inviting ideation and debate. The constantly shifting social materialities offered a sense of momentum and endless possibilities. Bricolage brought with it affective intensities, unorthodox organising and a new vocabulary of collaboration and innovation. However, although space providers gave permission to utilise space in relatively unbounded ways, members first needed to learn how to negotiate those spaces with each other.

As in any shared space, new coworkers can learn organisational norms and gain a sense of belonging by observing and practicing basic communal routines and rituals, like loading the dishwasher, not disturbing those wearing headphones,[2] booking meeting spaces using the calendar provided, and switching the lights off when you're last to leave. Shared understandings of such symbolic interactions foster a collegiality that maintains orderly use of a space and respect for each other's different uses of it. We learn such ordinary practices through legitimate peripheral participation (Lave, 1991). It is a form of situated learning, conventionally experienced in apprenticeships as gaining discrete knowledge of complex tasks by observing others' work and ways of being, and practicing to develop one's own ways of doing the same work. It is experiential learning – being shown rather than being told. Shared practices shape identities via a process that gives structure and meaning to knowledgeable skill from which Jean Lave and Etienne Wenger developed the communities of practice model (Lave, 1991). To become an accepted member of a community of practice requires participation in the technologies of everyday practices as well as social relations, production processes and activities (Lave and Wenger, 1991). New members learn what is acceptable and what is not through observation from the periphery of a community before practicing established routines and rituals that engender acceptance (after Handley *et al.*, 2007). However, entrées are first required, which in coworking is a key task performed by a central employee, the space host.

It is well-established that coworking space hosts are employed to create a sense of belonging and encourage active participation, often called community curation (Brown, 2017; Garrett, Spreitzer and Bacevice, 2017; Merkel, 2015). Hosts commonly have a desk near the entrance and are the first person you are likely to meet on any given day. They typically provide inductions, introduce members to each other and maintain a calendar of events. The skill of hosting is thought to facilitate but not lead community encounters such as weekly mixed bag lunches, seminars by invited speakers and wellbeing classes. They are the trim tabs of coworking.

Mixed bag lunches are particularly effective in generating a sense of community that is inclusive, convivial and member-driven – a key feature of the coworking space I regularly coworked at Melbourne in its early days. Individual members would bring ingredients to prepare meals together and share at the scheduled event each Thursday (Butcher, 2018). These straightforward regular events connected members through food preparation and housekeeping practices, inviting casual conversation and enabling announcements about individual achievements and upcoming events. Scheduled to occur immediately after open house events, in which potential new coworkers would receive a guided tour of the space, mixed bag lunches were curated to give structure and routine to informal networking opportunities. A communal ethos was symbolised to forge new connections, reinforce ordinary yet taken-for-granted tasks like cleaning the kitchen, and demonstrate to newcomers the convivialities of coworking. It did though take time and persistence for the space host to embed and hand over the basic organisational practices that ensured enough members would attend and contribute equitably and enthusiastically. Giving permission to members to take a lead in curation proved important, and over time members developed ways to organise, such as sending invites and maintaining lists of ingredients using social apps, that wouldn't detract from their daily work.

The key to such member-driven organising proved to be when members saw such mundane acts as being valued by others and reciprocated. Where some members might organise seminars or run clubs, others might bake cakes for mixed bag lunches or provide technical support for events. In other words, exchange value in trading skills and knowledge was found through learning what we each might best contribute to the community. What is relevant to the earlier argument in this book is that members performed particular community tasks or provided specific services, and from those became known for contributing certain things, thereby gaining the potential to create individual surplus value within the internal economy of a coworking community. For example, tax accountants might offer in-kind ad hoc advice, which may or may not lead to gaining new clients. Or an app developer in need of a brand identity might commission a graphic designer in exchange for free access to the app. These forms of gift-giving are common forms of social exchange found not only in entrepreneurial networks (Ferrary, 2003) but understood anthropologically as fundamental means of circulatory human interaction that have no explicit expectation of payment or immediate return (Mauss, 1990/1925, cited in Scott, 2009). Hence, compared with discrete monetary transactions for services, such exchanges are understood not as a form of capital extraction from the community but as a giving back to something or someone we feel we have benefited from (Butcher, 2018). Gift-giving engenders the trust and reciprocity that necessarily underpins legitimate peripheral participation.

Most fundamentally what is learned through peripheral participation in the everyday practices and convivialities of coworking is that equitable contributions to its organisation foster a sense of self intrinsically connected to others (Butcher, 2018). Such exchanges are necessary to co-curate the social relations in a coworking space that can enable the potential for collaboration. Learning to cowork is just the first stage in the process.

In 2018 while producing a series of short educational films on coworking, I met Rachel, who is an illustrator and, at the time of the interview in 2019, was a part-time space host at a London coworking space. Rachel described to me what she learned through coworking.

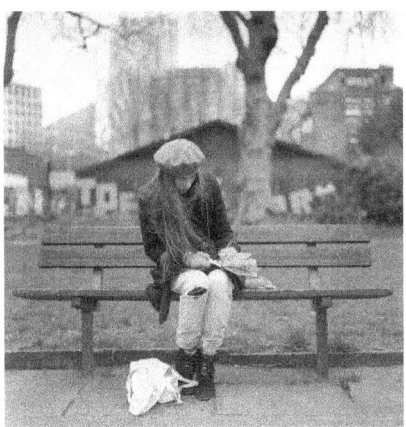

Image credit: Tim Butcher

'I remember someone the other day was saying "I don't think I could [freelance], I don't think I'd have the discipline to do it;" and I, kind of when I wasn't doing it properly, was thinking that myself. And it's one of those things where it's . . . I'm probably not doing it properly, but it's easier than it seems and you kinda just do things when you need to, and you do find that you have those inner reserves – it's really hard if you do it on your own, and then it is really hard to do anything. But when you do have other people around you, you do suddenly find that "I can do that, I can fill out a tax return; I can turn up 9 to 5, I can meet this deadline," and it just becomes more manageable.'

'I've taken on quite small commissions and so there tends to be more freedom in them – like how I do things, and how they look. But they also tend to be things I'm interested in as well. . . . I like them because you get to know other people really well through them and to know their experience of things.'

Rachel's comments suggest two important benefits of being actively connected with a coworking community. Firstly, Rachel's comments about self-discipline point to motivation that can be derived from observing how others practice seemingly mundane work tasks that we might find difficult without such peripheral participation. Secondly, Rachel's reference to taking on small commissions refers to her gaining some of those from other coworkers. Illustrators can pick up plenty of work in coworking spaces from freelancers and startups needing to enhance their visual identities. Connectedness brings with it learning how to work that can lead to opportunities for more work.

Coworking to learn

Empowering coworkers to co-curate situated learning experiences is central to my conceptualisation of coworking as a catalyst of collaboration (Butcher, 2018). Through legitimate peripheral participation, not only everyday organisational tasks are learned but understandings of each others' interests and motivations are gained. When that is coupled with permission to reconfigure space, orthodox ideas can be deconstructed and contested (Beyes and Michels, 2011; Bureau and Komporozos-Athanasiou, 2016; Bissola, Imperatori and Biffi, 2017). Reimagining space can invite challenge and playfulness to rethink and remake how we learn and work (Bissola, Imperatori and Biffi, 2017: Hjorth, 2005). Similarly, the materialities of Tom Sachs' studio invite playful bricolage to make art, while its 'ten bullet' rules maintain shared understandings of what is and isn't possible (mainly for health and safety reasons). The sort of attunement to practice that Sachs applies invites what Michel De Certeau (2011) calls tactical contestations of routines and rituals and understandings of self. Equally, what flexible coworking spaces can enable are safe spaces in which to reimagine self, test ideas and try new things before tactically deploying them in the wider world (Butcher, 2018).

In public entrepreneurship, Daniel Hjorth (2013) identifies a common desire to change not only society but to transform the process of social change. Desire for societal transformation is found to be the catalyst embodied by enterprising collectives seeking alternatives to the current hegemony, in response to the ongoing crises of neoliberalism and austerity politics (Daskalaki, Hjorth and Mair, 2015; Hjorth, 2013; Kokkinidis, 2015; Martí and Fernandez, 2015). Deeply situated projects and micro-political events from self-organised community centres and guerrilla gardening (see Daskalaki, 2018) to worker-occupied factories (see Kokkanidis, 2015) are organised to explore alternative socio-economic and socio-spatial formations that both contest present precarities and resist fixed, individualised, professional identities (Daskalaki, 2018; Kauppinen and Daskalaki, 2015). While Daskalaki (2018) finds spontaneity and ephemerality in communities repurposing public spaces, Kokkinidis (2015) sees worker collectives as promoting an ethic of care for one another. Arguably, such commonly felt desires well up in the bodies of such collectives so intensely that they feel compelled to act. As Brian Massumi suggests:

> the expression of affect, far from being anything goes, is an expression of necessity. . . . Affect assumes necessity, in the strong sense of taking it on. It takes it on in such a way as to extract from it a surplus-value of creativity.
>
> (2015, p. 208)

So, in public entrepreneurship, collectively shared affective responses to political crises, economic uncertainties, and individual precarities are mobilised as creative desires to understand and demonstrate how macro-level transformation might occur through micro-level collective action, in ways not dissimilar to the community arts movement.

Similarly, but more overtly entrepreneurial than political, ideas and innovations in coworking are not just a consequence of the spatial aesthetics or social relations, but how these are bricolaged in unorthodox ways. The production and practice of possibilities require more than a flexible space, trust and reciprocity. Whiteboards on wheels signify opportunities for ideation, while gift giving builds human connections, but these are just antecedents to collaboration. Permission to bricolage is necessary for coworkers with different interests and motivations to realise they share similar intentionalities, to help each other to develop and test whatever it is they are working on, or even to spin off into new collaborations on new projects (e.g. building a start-up, developing social innovations or a political campaign) (Butcher, 2018). Through events such as mixed bag lunches, changemaker workshops, and post-work discussions around whiteboards, I have witnessed not only ideation but a lexicon of collaboration developed in coworking spaces. 'Curating community,' 'getting shit done' and 'cultivating ideas' were just some of the discursive motifs that I found transferred from workshops and seminars to informal gatherings and became embedded in everyday conversation or found their way onto stickers, t-shirts and mugs. That language and the practices they represent also move from space to space, as coworkers connect digitally across global networks and move between spaces when travelling. Legitimate peripheral participation in coworking – being in the space, observing others' practices and picking up the vocabulary – not only engenders a sense of community but, when catalysed by highly motivated people who project clear intentionalities, can become so much more than just working together alone (Butcher, 2018).

Many of the events I participated in at spaces in Melbourne and London were designed to share unorthodox contestational ideas and purposefully use those spaces in uncanny ways to stimulate debate and generate affective intensities to foster a shared sense of intentionality. Workshops presented diverse yet connected ideas from how to become a changemaker to how to cope with life as a freelancer. Spaces were curated to build up affective atmospheres that heightened emotions, invited critical questioning and generated ideas and suggestions. This was a time when the TED Talk genre was exploding and crowdfunding was gaining momentum. The pitching of disruptive ideas and innovations was in its prime, and many coworkers sought to learn how. Coworkers could make and use the platforms they co-created to get feedback on ideas, hone pitches and rehearse presentations before taking them out onto the open stage and into the wider market in search of investment (Butcher, 2018). Hence, when members feel empowered to collaborate and perform their contestational intentionalities and identities, coworking spaces become important interstices between the generation of ideas and realisation of their potential. Legitimate peripheral participation can extend beyond shared everyday rituals and gift giving to learning from each other how to communicate unorthodox ideas and practices in acceptable ways, while developing and practicing unique professional identities. In my research, I have observed coworkers not only learning from each other how to tactically contest orthodoxy but also, more fundamentally, how to develop the self-efficacy they needed to action their intentionalities (Butcher, 2018).

From affective intensities to conscious intentionalities

Such intentionalities, typically talked about as changemaking, were how many of the coworkers I encountered expressed and acted on their desires to create unique entrepreneurial identities, novel working practices and new products or services. However, 'entrepreneur' was then a moniker few chose to adopt. Experimentation and bricolage were typically enacted spontaneously and ephemerally. Even coffee catch-ups provided ways to connect with new people, test out ideas and practice intentionalities (Butcher, 2018). Clark and Holt (2010) find entrepreneurial intentionalities expressed as an ethic of breaking free of conventions, imaginative creation and self-legitimising maxims, established through reflective judgement based on social performance, public challenge and personal autonomy. More broadly, intentionalities are discrete yet explicit everyday acts that needn't be entrepreneurial. We all set intentions and goals to achieve things every day. Intentionalities are not extraordinary, so we tend to take them for granted. However, they are fundamental to action. It is therefore important for the argument of this book to understand intentionality conceptually in order to appreciate the process of transforming pre-conscious affective intensities and critical consciousness discussed in Chapter 3 into meaningful action. In other words, for example, how the bricolage convivialities of coworking are converted into entrepreneurial or political action.

Etymologically, intentionality is derived from the Latin: *intentio*, from the verb *intendere*: to be directed towards some goal or thing (Jacob, 2003). Philosophically, Edmund Husserl develops the ideas of his mentor, Franz Brentano, by employing this notion of intentionality in motion, to develop a philosophy of beginnings – phenomenology – in order to understand consciousness and how we construct meaning (Freeman, 2021). Jean-Paul Sartre quotes Husserl's notion that 'all consciousness is consciousness of something'; to know is to 'burst towards' (1970, p. 5). Sartre therefore suggests that this 'of-ness' is important in understanding what makes an intention an act and a movement towards something (after Smith and McIntyre, 1982). So, intentionality is therefore central to phenomenology, in that it enables us to understand how our bodies convert consciousness into action. It is the missing piece of our conceptual framework.

Phenomenologically, consciousness and intentionality are understood as being not just cognitive but relational – they are intersubjective, embodied, sensory experiences, not confined to the mind but felt through our bodies (after Donohoe, 2016). Intentionality is for Maurice Merleau-Ponty how we attune ourselves to lived experience (Willems, 2018). If we want to understand the felt experiences of a phenomenon, we need to appreciate how bodies perceive those experiences through the senses. Interpreted from Merleau-Ponty's *Phenomenology of Perception*, Baldwin (2008/2004) suggests:

> It is our 'bodily' intentionality which brings the possibility of meaning into our experience by ensuring that its content, the things presented in experience, are surrounded with references to the past and future, to other places and other things, to human possibilities and situations.

Merleau-Ponty helps us to understand the connectedness of our experience of things (Baldwin, 2004/2008). 'Bodily intentionality brings the possibility of meaning into our experience' (Ménasé, in Merleau-Ponty, 2008, p. 9). So, through learning to act intentionally, coworkers reflexively draw on the intersubjectivities of their individual pasts and collective presents to convert their ideas into meaningful action. Curated legitimate peripheral participation and playful bricolage, as in the other collectives discussed, mobilises individual pre-conscious affective intensities through shared dialogue that produces a critical consciousness towards intentions to do something meaningful. For example, where common feelings of precarity exist, dialogues that draw on those feelings might make conscious the ideological forces or social injustices that cause such unsettling sensations, thereby generating intentionalities to take action to address the root causes of the problem.

Public or social entrepreneurship practices found in spaces like coworking agonistically blur the lines between political and entrepreneurial intentionalities by playing with discursive ambiguities. Pre-conscious affects store up in the body to create manifold potentialities (Brown and Reavey, 2015), and here we see language and practices being learned and developed to consciously act on affect, based on the discursive resources available. Husserl shows that an intentionality directed towards something is not contingent on the existence of that thing, and so we act independently of whether it is real or not (Jacob, 2003).[3] And so discursive devices like curation and changemaking do not need to be real to draw out affects and generate intentions to act. What is important is that they are deployed with critical consciousness. Dialogue in spaces like coworking or worker collectives is far more likely to generate criticality than if we work in isolation. Shared entrepreneurial intentionalities need not be depoliticised. Potentialities lie in learning a collective identity of *we* derived from passionate affective investment (Mouffe, 2013).

Notes

1 Knolling is a term adopted by Sachs, first used by Andrew Kromelow in 1987, a janitor at Frank Gehry's furniture fabrication shop (where Sachs worked at the time), to define a routine of arranging tools at right-angles on workbenches to organise the space (Wikipedia, n.d.).
2 Wearing headphones while working is a symbolic act that signifies not wanting to be disturbed – a straightforward and unconfrontational way of communicating this, commonly accepted in coworking.
3 Subsequently, Bertrand Russell solves this problem via his mathematical proof, the theory of definite descriptions (Jacob, 2003), and John Searle extends the concept by illustrating the distinction between being conscious and simulating by arguing that the human brain is distinctly conscious because it can consider the meaning of things (Searle, 1983/1999).

References

Baldwin, T. (2004/2008) 'Introduction', in Merleau-Ponty, M. (ed.) *The World of perception*. Abingdon: Routledge, pp. 1–28.
Benterrak, K., Muecke, S. and Roe, P. (1984/1996) *Reading the country*. South Freemantle, AU: Freemantle Arts Centre Press.

Beyes, T. and Michels, C. (2011) 'The production of educational space: Heterotopia and the business university', *Management Learning*, 42(5), pp. 521–536. https://doi.org/10.1177/1350507611400001.

Bissola, R., Imperatori, B. and Biffi, A. (2017) 'A rhizomatic learning process to create collective knowledge in entrepreneurship education: Open innovation and collaboration beyond boundaries', *Management Learning*, 48(2), pp. 206–226. https://doi.org/10.1177/1350507616672735.

Brown, J. (2017) 'Curating the "third place"? Coworking and the mediation of creativity', *Geoforum*, 82, pp. 112–126. https://doi.org/10.1016/j.geoforum.2017.04.006.

Brown, S. and Reavey, P. (2015) *Vital memory and affect: Living with a difficult past.* Hove: Routledge.

Bureau, S.P. and Komporozos-Athanasiou, A. (2016) 'Learning subversion in the business school: An "improbable" encounter', *Management Learning*, 48(1), pp. 39–56. https://doi.org/10.1177/1350507616661262.

Butcher, T. (2018) 'Learning everyday entrepreneurial practices through coworking', *Management Learning*, 49(3), pp. 327–345. https://doi.org/10.1177/1350507618757088.

Clarke, J. and Holt, R. (2010) 'Reflective judgement: Understanding entrepreneurship as ethical practice', *Journal of Business Ethics*, 94(3), pp. 317–331. Available at: www.jstor.org/stable/40784697.

Daskalaki, M. (2018) 'Alternative organizing in times of crisis: Resistance assemblages and socio-spatial solidarity', *European Urban and Regional Studies*, 25(2), 155pp. –170. https://doi.org/10.1177/0969776416683001.

Daskalaki, M., Hjorth, D. and Mair, J. (2015) 'Are entrepreneurship, communities, and social transformation related?' *Journal of Management Inquiry*, 24(4), pp. 419–423. https://doi.org/10.1177/1056492615579012.

De Certeau, M. (2011) *The practice of everyday life.* Berkeley, CA: University of California Press.

Derrida, J. (1970/2014) 'Structure, sign and play in the discourse of the human sciences', in Lodge, D. and Wood, N. (eds.) *Modern criticism and theory: A reader.* New York, NT: Routledge.

Donohoe, J. (2016) *Husserl on ethics and intersubjectivity: From static to genetic phenomenology.* Toronto: University of Toronto Press.

Ferrary, M. (2003) 'The gift exchange in the social networks of Silicon Valley', *California Management Review*, 45(4), pp. 120–138.

Freeman, M. (2021) 'Five threats to phenomenology's distinctiveness', *Qualitative Inquiry*, 27(2), pp. 276–282. https://doi.org/10.1177/1077800420912799.

Garrett, L.E., Spreitzer, G.M. and Bacevice, P.A. (2017) 'Co-constructing a sense of community at work: The emergence of community in coworking spaces', *Organization Studies*, 38(6), pp. 821–842. https://doi.org/10.1177/0170840616685354.

Handley, K., Clark, T., Fincham, R., *et al.* (2007) 'Researching situated learning: Participation, identity and practices in client – consultant relationships', *Management Learning*, 38(2), pp. 173–191. https://doi.org/10.1177/1350507607075774.

Hjorth, D. (2005) 'Organizational entrrrpreneurship: With de Certeau on creating heterotopias (or spaces for play)', *Journal of Management Inquiry*, 14(4), pp. 386–398. https://doi.org/10.1177/1056492605280225.

Hjorth, D. (2013) 'Public entrepreneurship: Desiring social change, creating sociality', *Entrepreneurship and Regional Development*, 25(1–2), pp. 34–51. https://doi.org/10.1080/08985626.2012.746883.

Jacob, P. (2003) 'Intentionality', in *The Stanford encyclopedia of philosophy*. Available at: https://plato.stanford.edu/entries/intentionality/ (Accessed: 17 February 2023).

Kauppinen, A. and Daskalaki, M. (2015) 'Becoming other: Entrepreneurship as subversive organising', *Ephemera: Theory and Politics in Organization*, 15(3), pp. 601–620. https://ephemerajournal.org/contribution/%25E2%2580%2598becoming-other%25E2%2580%2599-entrepreneuring-subversive-organising.

Kokkinidis, G. (2015) 'Post-capitalist imaginaries: The case of workers' collectives in Greece', *Journal of Management Inquiry*, 24(4), pp. 429–432. https://doi.org/10.1177/1056492615579788.

Lave, J. (1991) 'Situated learning in communities of practice', in Resnick, L.B., Levine, J.M. and Teasley, S.D. (eds.) *Perspectives on socially shared cognition*. Washington, DC: American Psychological Association, 63–82.

Lave, J. and Wenger, E. (1991) *Situated learning: Legitimate peripheral participation in communities of practice*. Cambridge: Cambridge University Press.

Martí, I. and Fernandez, P. (2015) 'Entrepreneurship, togetherness and emotions: A look at (post-crisis?) Spain', *Journal of Management Inquiry*, 24(4), pp. 424–428. https://doi.org/10.1177/1056492615579786.

Massumi, B. (2015) *Politics of affect*. Cambridge: Polity Press.

Merkel, J. (2015) 'Coworking in the city', *Ephemera: Theory and Politics in Organization*, 15(1), pp. 121–139. https://ephemerajournal.org/contribution/coworking-city.

Ménasé, S. (2008) 'Foreword', in Merleau-Ponty, M. (ed.) *The world of perception*. Abingdon: Routledge, pp. vii–viii.

Mouffe, C. (2013) *Agonistics: Thinking the world politically*. London: Verso. eBook: eISBN 9781781682357.

Sachs, T. (2010) *Ten bullets*. Available at: www.youtube.com/watch?v=49p1JVLHUos (Accessed: 17 February 2023).

Sachs, T. (2011) *Color*. Available at: www.youtube.com/watch?v=eBM_9W_e_D4 (Accessed: 17 February 2023).

Sachs, T. (2012) *Love letter to plywood*. Available at: www.youtube.com/watch?v=pVxldyIa0Bg (Accessed: 17 February 2023).

Sartre, J-P. (1970) 'Intentionality: A fundamental idea of Husserl's phenomenology', *Journal of the British Society for Phenomenology*, 1(2), 4–5. DOI: 10.1080/00071773.1970.11006118.

Searle, J. (1983/1999) *Intentionality: An essay in the philosophy of mind*. Cambridge: Cambridge University Press.

Scott, S. (2009) *Making sense of everyday life*. Cambridge: Polity Press.

Smith, D.W. and McIntyre, R. (1982) *Husserl and intentionality: A study of mind, meaning and language*. Dordrecht: D. Reidel Publishing. ISBN: 978-94-010-9383-5.

Sperone Wastewater. (n.d.) *American bricolage, exhibition catalogue*. Sperone Westwater, New York 2 November–22 December 2000. Available at: www.speronewestwater.com/exhibitions/american-bricolage#tab:slideshow (Accessed: 17 February 2023).

Spinuzzi, C. (2012) 'Working alone together coworking as emergent collaborative activity', *Journal of Business and Technical Communication*, 26(4), pp. 399–441. https://doi.org/10.1177/1050651912444070.

Studio 368 (n.d.) *368 Resume*. Available at: www.368.nyc (Accessed: 17 February 2023).

van de Walle, M. (n.d.) *Tom Sachs: Biography*. Available at: www.tomsachs.com/biography (Accessed: 17 February 2023).

Waters-Lynch, J., Potts, J., Butcher, T., Dodson, J. and Hurley, J. (2016) *Coworking: A transdisciplinary overview*. Available at: https://papers.ssrn.com/sol3/papers.cfm?abstract_id=2712217 accessed 17/2/ 2023.

Wikipedia. (n.d.) *Tom Sachs*. Available at: https://en.wikipedia.org/wiki/Tom_Sachs (Accessed: 17 February 2023).

Willems, T. (2018) 'Seeing and sensing the railways: A phenomenological view on practice-based learning', *Management Learning*, 49(1), pp. 23–39. https://doi.org/10.1177/1350507617725188

5 Socially engaged learning

The politics of cultural democracy

> Consciousness is no longer the mere product of social being but is at once a
> condition of its practical existence and, further, one of its central productive forces.
> (Williams, 1980/2020, p. 287)

Here, Raymond Williams articulates an understanding akin to the phenomenological conceptualisation of making consciousness actionable through
intentionality discussed in Chapter 4, juxtaposed against more orthodox
understandings of consciousness that draw on the Cartesian logic of 'I think
therefore I am.' In science, we still do not have a rational scientific explana-
tion for *how* consciousness works (Seth, 2021), but in phenomenology, we
don't need one. Instead, what can be drawn out of the coworking case is that
if we can connect with other people with shared interests or concerns, and we
learn how to work together, we might make conscious our affective desires to
act on them intentionally. Pre-consciousness, consciousness and intentionality
make up an embodied, moving process – a process of becoming, as opposed
to simply being (Probyn, 1996). So, collectively making conscious the affective intensities held in our bodies and putting them to work can yield the
production and practice of possibilities envisaged by Williams. While we do
so within the current neoliberal hegemony those intensities are most likely
channelled through entrepreneurial intentionalities, but they need not necessarily be individualised projects of self. Instead, as I have experienced in coworking, shared intentionalities can be collectively enacted. Social, political
and entrepreneurial intentionalities are melded together through bricolage and
play with discursive ambiguities to create possibility.

In this chapter, we return to socially engaged art and the concept of cultural democracy to see how through purposeful pedagogical approaches,
shared arts practices can generate affective intensities, and agonistically make
us conscious of specific social injustices and political issues, to engender
intentionalities to address them. What will be shown is how contemporary

DOI: 10.4324/9781003162025-5

arts-based situated learning encounters can be curated to foster intentionalities towards cultural democracy.

Socially engaged art was introduced in Chapter 2 as a specific form of participatory art informed by the politics and practices of the 1970s community arts movement, which were absorbed into the creative economy to promote social inclusion of marginalised groups (Belfiore, 2021; Hope, 2017). Froggett et al. suggest that the barriers to participation in the arts are psychological for many people, citing self-exclusionary talk in which those who are marginalised in society feel art is, for example, 'not for them' (2011, p. 91). Socially engaged art borrows from non-arts-based participatory practices ranging from psychotherapy and social care to education and community development. The act of taking part in collective artmaking enables the discovery of new ways of feeling that connect people: 'when aesthetic form is found to "contain" otherwise inchoate or inexpressible feeling, it can become a "force" – that "moves" individuals or becomes a driver of social change' (Froggett *et al.*, 2011, p. 91, emphasis in original). As discussed in Chapter 2, socially engaged art navigates the creative economy discourse of investment in both non-commercial artists and particular social groups. Socially engaged art is a form of creative work that legitimately aims to demonstrate social inclusion while achieving cultural democracy.

Cultural democracy invites affirmation, expression and questioning of one's own and other's values and the relationship between them (Matarasso, 2019). Conceptually, it is understood as a form of direct participation in dialogue to contest constraints on marginalised groups' cultural production in the present by imagining alternative futures (Jeffers, 2017; Kelly, Lock and Merkel, 1986). In Gramscian terms, where the dominant hegemony serves to marginalise the cultural understandings and practices of particular groups, the egalitarian ideal of cultural democracy invites a critical consciousness of specific inequalities and injustices and consideration of alternative hegemonies.

Where social inclusion is commonly an explicit and measurable aim of socially engaged projects, cultural democracy is arguably an implicit leitmotif that complements it. The logic and discourse of social inclusion is normative – its objective is conformance to social norms (Alacovska, 2020; Belfiore, 2021). This implies that socially engaged art should therefore also be normative. However, ambiguities in social inclusion discourse, such as recognising diversity and equality facilitate critical interpretation. This is not to suggest that socially engaged art is subversive, but that it can achieve significant outcomes that enable marginalised groups to not only feel included but also listened to, understood and supported. Cultural democracy is not the antithesis of social inclusion but perhaps its critical conscience.

Cultural democracy ideals directly inform socially engaged arts workers' and artists' career choices and their commitments to project participants (Jeffers, 2017). Broadly speaking, artists' individual experiences of marginalisation, disadvantage, inequality or injustice motivate them to follow this precarious career path. I have interviewed socially engaged artists from working-class, migrant backgrounds who have shared with me not only their experiences but also those of their parents and grandparents, which inform their arts practices. Socially engaged art is deeply meaningful work rooted in self-care and mutual support. So much so that Ana Alacovska (2020) has conceptualised socially engaged arts work as a form of care work, as introduced in Chapter 2. When working directly with groups who feel excluded from mainstream institutions such as healthcare and education, socially engaged artists and arts workers are able to offer care and support or identify care needs not otherwise noticed (Alacovska, 2020). As Dowling notes: 'caring for and about what one does and the people one does it for (paradoxically) becomes a way of protecting oneself from feelings of alienation or despondency' (2021, p. 39). Alacovska goes further to argue that such mutuality, responsibility and commitment extends to concerns for project participants' achievement of 'certain standards of social justice, wellbeing, healing and emancipation' (2020, p. 733).

I met Isabel in 2019. Isabel is an academic and artist who researches and practices socially engaged art. Isabel told me about her life history of intergenerational migration, which informs her practice and care for project participants with similar experiences. Isabel doesn't just make art with participants but invites dialogue through sharing cultural practices. Through ordinary shared making practices like sewing or woodworking, participants work towards a defined project outcome that benefits their community. This process opens up conversations about common everyday struggles, such as access to public services – normal everyday things most people take for granted, but marginalised people need assistance with to understand how to comply with bureaucratic processes.

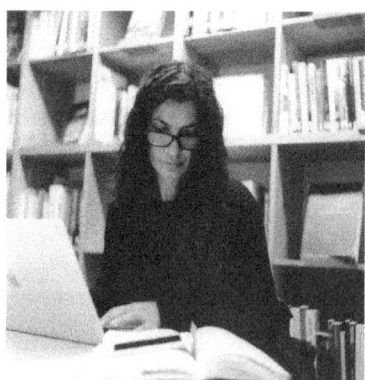

Image credit: Tim Butcher

'All the work that I do is just the one practice. It takes many different forms and shapes, and the way that it is easiest to describe it is
socially engaged art, just because it gives me the freedom to go into
any different direction that I might want.'
   'But more recently I'm trying to find a way that I can define my
practice without using the 'socially engaged art' words, and I think
that this has just got to do with the reaction from what I've seen –
our methodologies or artists' ways of working being appropriated
by those in power, and co-opted. Because of that, I want to distance
myself from the terminology. Not necessarily the work that I'm
doing, but the terminology.'
   'If I want to work in solidarity with different groups of people
to achieve certain kinds of outcomes that usually go against those
in power, I can't really be using the same kind of terminology as
they are.'
   'The most difficult thing, it's not the work, . . . it's because of the
people that you work with. You're fully getting into their lives and
they're getting fully into your life – it becomes an intense process,
because it is not just a relationship of artist or participant. . . . It goes
to the most basic level, which is the one-to-one relation to another
human, and that requires a lot of effort and energy – a lot of energy.'

Pedagogy and dialogue

Isabel's embeddedness in the lives of project participants reflects her care
for them and is indicative of a critical pedagogical approach. As discussed in
Chapter 2, the making of art in socially engaged projects serves as an aesthetic
third (Froggett *et al.*, 2011). The socio-materialities of making something
generate dialogue through which participant-produced, socially inclusive
outcomes can be produced *and* space is made for participants to feel cared
about and their contributions listened to. The value of socially engaged arts
projects lies in the condition and character of their dialogical exchanges (Kester, 2012). Dialogue is more important than what is made; and the aesthetic
qualities of the process inform the quality of the dialogue. Hence pedagogical
approaches have become pivotal to the success of socially engaged art. However, it was not until the mid-2000s that participatory art began to formally
explore the relationship between art and pedagogy (Bishop, 2012). Importantly, the pedagogical turn enables arts-based encounters to be conveyed to
audiences in relatable ways (Bishop, 2012) and demonstrates legitimacy to
investors (Belfiore, 2015).
   Pedagogical design of such encounters gives structure and meaning to dialogue, which not only legitimises project outcomes but also invites critical

consciousness through which participants feel free to reimagine their current situations and future possibilities. For example, Isabel told me about the Gresham Wooden Horse project, that brought together disparate communities in the Gresham area of Middlesborough, UK to co-produce a neighbourhood plan via a series of workshops. Isabel led this socially engaged arts project. The motif of the Trojan horse from Ancient Greek mythology provided an aesthetic third through which the plan could be discussed and developed by participants from different cultural backgrounds and then communicated by them to the public. The co-design and construction of a large-scale wooden horse and it being taken through the streets of Gresham served as a vehicle to generate public awareness and engagement in the plan, and its DIY aesthetic and scale reflect longitudinal community commitment to the neighbourhood (O'Brien, 2022). As Kester (2012) argues, socially engaged art aims to develop legitimate shared provisional understandings rather than universally binding decisions. The dialogical aesthetic of co-creating socially engaged art is one of openness, listening, willingness to accept dependence, and intersubjective vulnerability (Kester, 2012). When designed with coherent, robust participation philosophies for sustained engagement, such learning encounters can have a vitality that enriches cultural exchange (Alacovska, 2020; Froggett *et al.*, 2011).

Such participatory, action-oriented and politically situated forms of social inquiry through aesthetic practices are widely understood as critical arts pedagogy, and the bedrock of socially engaged art (Bishop, 2012; Finley, Vonk and Finley, 2014). Open and inclusive dialogue holds potential for the transformative agency necessary to identify and confront systemic oppressions, target sites of resistance, and map possibilities for transformative practice (Finley, Vonk and Finley, 2014; Wright, 2020). It speaks to an idea discussed in Chapter 4 that through permission to reconfigure space, orthodox ideas can be deconstructed and contested (Beyes and Michels, 2011; Bureau and Komporozos-Athanasiou, 2016; Bissola, Imperatori and Biffi, 2017). While implicit in the idea of cultural democracy, 'conscientisation' or the process of becoming critical consciousness is explicit in critical arts pedagogy (Mernick, 2021, p. 19; after Friere, 1970). Besides Isabel's work, critical pedagogy is also evident in Bern's art (see Chapter 2) that raises awareness of social injustices such as the deaths of thousands of refugees fleeing persecution through her project, *Dead Reckoning* and is embedded in Richard's performance art that invites critical questioning of, for example, the privatisation of public space (see Chapter 3).

Fundamentally, different cultural experiences and readings of experience produce contestations over meanings (Cuddy-Keane, 2003). Practical engagement with cultural materialities can educate and facilitate direct participation (Williams, 1961). However, Raymond Williams understands this as an extended dialogical process of discrete context-specific collective acts of learning (see Williams, 1980/2020, 1961). He does not see systemic transformation any time soon, but instead a continuous process of specific and changing relationships with culture that offers hope for cultural revolution (Williams, 1980/2020). Longitudinal projects such as the Gresham Wooden Horse can produce and practice significant community-level possibilities, but arguably not enough for systemic transformation on a larger scale – a point also made by Gramsci (c.1933/1986). Nevertheless, what this form of socially engaged art project embodies is a pedagogy that can invoke affective intensities through a dialogical aesthetic sufficient to produce agonistic dialogue (Mouffe, 2013). Such projects not only offer care and support in the present but are generative of relationalities necessary to continue the dialogue.

The following case studies will show how by bringing together different socially engaged arts projects or sharing critical pedagogical practices, a continuous, less site-specific dialogue might be generated.

Who are We?

Who are We? was a three-year project produced by Counterpoints Arts in partnership with The Open University from 2017 to 2019. It was a cross-platform socially engaged arts programme, spanning the various arts practices to critically explore citizenship and migration (Colom, 2019; Who are we? n.d.a). Different projects were commissioned each year and curated into three annual five-day exhibitions at Tate Exchange, a dedicated free space for community engagement at Tate Modern in London.[1] Each project was situated in the exhibition space or interfaced with it online for the week of the exhibition as either an installation or live performance through which members of the public could interact with the art and artists. Each project was pedagogically designed as a unique learning encounter to provoke critical consciousness of citizenship and migration (Colom, 2019). Experienced together as a series of encounters in a single space, viewers could choose to become participants, if only for the short time they visited the exhibition.

My own involvement in *Who are We?* was to produce *Tales of Precarity* for the 2019 exhibition, a research project through which I met some of the artists in the vignettes of this book to co-curate visual stories of their experiences of work as socially engaged artists. I attended the 2019 exhibition and participated in some of the live projects throughout the week.

I recall deeply affective encounters through which I learned about refugees' experiences of migration through participation in aesthetic dialogues. One particularly poignant experience was with *As far as isolation goes*, a performance by musician and street artist, Basel Zaraa, and live artist, Tania El Khoury, about the health experiences of refugees in detention centres and the mental health system (see Who are we? n.d.b). It was positioned at the farthest point from the entrance – a quieter, peripheral space. I sat on a chair next to a wooden wall painted with blackboard paint, put on headphones

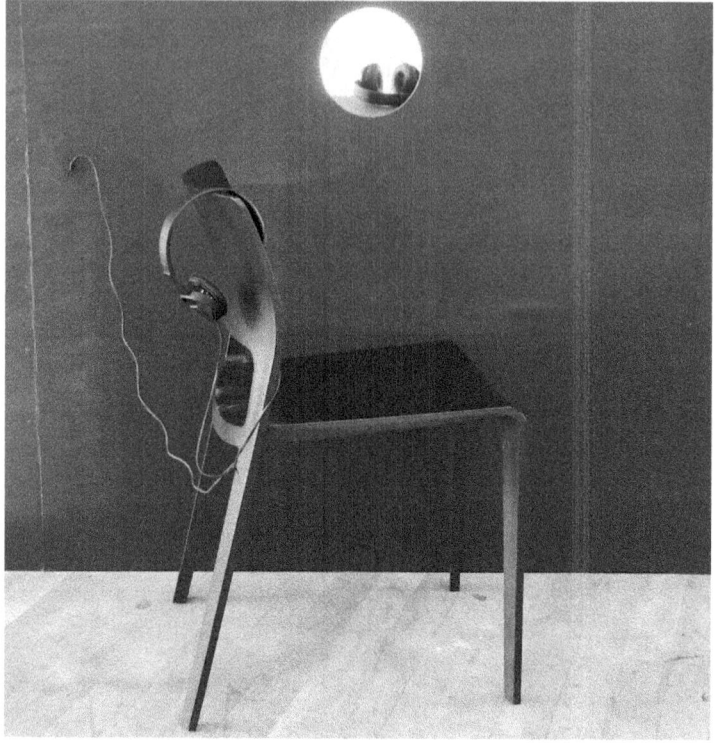

Figure 5.1 A chair and headphones, part of the *As far as isolation goes* art installation at *Who are We? 2019.*

Image credit: Tim Butcher

provided, rolled up my sleeve, and put my bare arm through a hole in a wall (see Figure 5.1).

I sensed the artist on the other side of that wall, who played pre-recorded sounds through the headphones and lightly touched my arm, but I couldn't make out quite what they were doing. Feelings of vulnerability in putting my arm through the hole were followed by my attempts to make sense of the unsettling sensations of whatever was happening to my arm. Virtually, it felt like it lasted longer than I'd expected, but in reality, was probably no more than three or four minutes. After the encounter, I withdrew my arm to find images drawn on my skin (see Figure 5.2). I was invited to write a reflection on my experience on the wall using chalk provided. In some sense, I learned what vulnerability feels like without being taught what refugees experience in institutions. It offered me enough insight to make me wonder how much

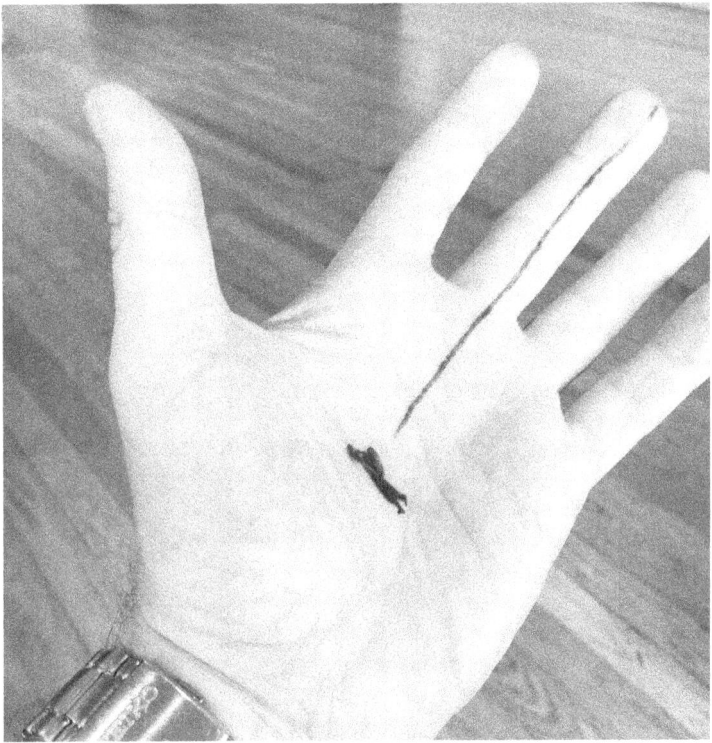

Figure 5.2 The author's hand, after being drawn on by the artist in the *As far as isolation goes* art installation at *Who are We? 2019*.

Image credit: Tim Butcher

more vulnerable refugees must feel each and every day. The experience was agonistically unsettling rather than antagonistically confronting.

Another project at the centre of the exhibition space was *Recognise – Risk – Reimagine – Rebuild – Redistribute* that sought to directly address cultural democracy (see Who are we? n.d.c). 17 visual, live art, spoken-word artists and dramaturges with diverse practices were commissioned to engage exhibition visitors in ideas for alleviating socio-economic divisions in society and building resilient, civic communities. On each day a different group of three to four artists led learning encounters to tackle each theme in turn (e.g. *Recognise* was engaged with on the first day of the exhibition, *Risk* on the second, and so on), to iteratively curate a series of dialogues that reflected on and added to what had been produced the previous day. Various materials and spaces in the Tate were used to generate dialogue. For example, where one group used drawing materials in the exhibition space, another went into other gallery spaces to engage participants in ideas about the value of the art in the permanent collection. The outcomes of each day's work were scribed on a blackboard – some artists invited participants to contribute directly to the blackboard themselves (see Figure 5.3). Each day's encounters were pedagogically informed and planned in advance; the artists having participated in a workshop a month earlier to discuss initial ideas before developing their collaborative approaches. Yet each artist was also open to the emergence of possibility, embracing how different participants engaged with the materials provided and building from the work done the previous day.

The final event of the 2019 exhibition was a gathering around the blackboard to reflect on the week-long project, discuss what was learned and

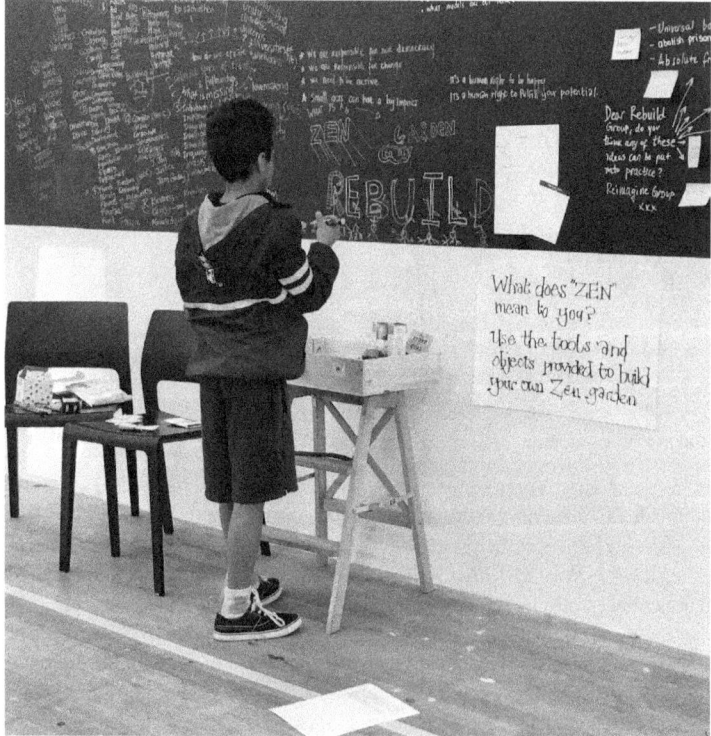

Figure 5.3 A child writing on the blackboard provided for the *Recognise – Risk – Reimagine – Rebuild – Redistribute* project at *Who are We? 2019.*

Image credit: Tim Butcher

consider what actions might arise from it. Based on five distinct yet complementary pedagogical designs that produced discrete, ephemeral participant encounters through each day of the exhibition, this project was not merely a means to engage and inform participants, but a series of activities generative of actionable dialogue. Intentionalities were drawn out of the curation of all of the weeks' creative encounters to generate ideas for future projects. As Raymond Williams suggests, the production and practice of possibilities is an ongoing body of work (1980/2020). Making space for specific aesthetic dialogues is crucial to generating critical consciousness, but in a world full of distractions those dialogues must be revisited and built on time and again to regenerate and sustain ideas and practices of cultural democracy.

Reclaim the archive

Another socially engaged arts project that I collaborated with Counterpoints Arts and The Tate on was *Reclaim the Archive*. Originally discussed and designed in late 2019, it was implemented in mid-2020 during the first UK lockdown of the COVID-19 pandemic. The immediate closures of arts spaces and events, constraints imposed on arts funding and physical distancing restrictions forced us to redesign what had been planned as an artistic intervention in the physical spaces of the Tate Archive in collaboration with Tate archive curators. We had planned to enable hip hop artists to investigate the archives in decolonial ways to produce work that would invite young people to reimagine arts institutions through public workshops and learning encounters, to break down virtual and real barriers to access to the arts. As Froggett *et al.* (2011) suggest, socially engaged art can de-mythologise and encourage access to the arts and other institutional spaces perceived as uninviting. Indicative of the broader trend of arts institutions to make their spaces more socially inclusive and educational (Matarasso, 2019), the Tate embraced the project.

Despite lockdown restrictions, the project team was able to salvage sufficient budget to run a redesigned first phase of the project and commission three artists, a dramaturge and web developers (see Butcher, 2021). This was at a time of extreme uncertainty for artists, arts workers, arts organisations and institutions. Counterpoints Arts reorganised its entire portfolio of projects, while each of us involved in the project was adapting to the instabilities of working from home and the insecurities of not knowing how long the lockdown would last. It was an immensely difficult time for everyone, and the project was redesigned to recognise this.

The project employs critical hip hop pedagogy. Chiara Minestrelli suggests that hip hop affords expression of identity and politics, but that it would be reductive to restrict a definition of the practice to an act of resistance (2017). For Minestrelli, hip hop is a practice of bricolage in the sense that Jacques Derrida understands it: 'if one calls bricolage the necessity of borrowing one's concept from the text of a heritage, which is more or less coherent or ruined, it must be said that every discourse is bricoleur' (Derrida, 1993; cited by Minestrelli, 2017, p. 5). Minestrelli also draws on Benterrak et al.'s definition of bricolage offered in Chapter 4 as 'roaming through the ruins of a culture,' which itself is taken from Derrida's definition, to show how hip hop is a critical practice that employs sampling, representin' and flow to create new sounds as a means of cultural revitalisation that is constantly evolving (Benterrak, Muecke and Roe, 1984/1996, p. 168, in Minestrelli, 2017, p. 5). Understood pedagogically, hip hop can place learners at the centre of a situation to turn their gaze towards their community and foster dialogue towards social change, offering a kind of radical hope for the future (Minestrelli, 2020). Hence, critical hip hop pedagogy is a practice through which (typically) marginalised young people not only listen to critical understandings of past and present oppression or disavowal of their cultures, but can actively participate in to develop their own understandings of their heritage and place in society, expressing their identities in creative ways.

With the imposed constraints of lockdown in place, the first phase of the project was made digital. Fortunately, many of the artefacts in the Tate Archive are available online. Although it could not offer the same sensory experience of being in and amongst artworks, the commissioned artists were able to search digitised images of particular work to explore what they could engage with and how they might respond to it.

Three hip hop artists were 'invited to speak back to and reimagine the idea of the archive, to insert new perspectives and retrieve silenced voices and cultural viewpoints' (Reclaim the Archive, n.d.). Shay D, AWATE and Big Zuu's commissions were in the form of residencies in which they collaborated with a Tate archive curator to research the work of artists they selected. As practitioner-researchers, Shay D, AWATE and Big Zuu were mentored by Hassan Mamadallie, a playwright and writer, whose project role was dramaturge. Hassan offered support and advice to the artists through Zoom calls – dialogues that deepened their critical inquiries. The website produced illustrates how together the artists reflected on the art and artists they were engaging with, their feelings about the work they were doing, and how they developed their intended responses (Reclaim the Archive, n.d.). Each artist engaged with specific artwork that they felt culturally meaningful to them. The music and videos produced from this first phase of the project represent not only the artists' own sense of identity but also their revelations about what is held in the archive. Their realisations that work of cultural significance to them are archived at the Tate opened up possibilities for further exploration and critical inquiry. Designed as a living archive, the website connects with social media to enable continued dialogue if/when the project moves into future phases of pedagogical engagement.

Curating dialogue

As found in coworking, curation is implicit in producing the dialogues necessary to draw out critical consciousness of affective experiences and generate intentions to act on them. Explicitly, critical pedagogy is central to curating socially engaged arts encounters, whereas coworking encounters are less formalised. While pedagogy provides legitimacy to socially engaged arts projects (Belfiore, 2015), it more importantly offers a structured approach to dialogue, directing it towards cultural democracy and producing possibilities to keep the conversation going. This generates not only possibilities for future funded projects that commission artists and support participants, but also builds towards the sorts of longitudinal exchanges that both Williams and Gramsci see as necessary. This is not to suggest socially engaged art is purposefully counter-hegemonic but that its pedagogical approach, similarly to the legitimate peripheral participation found in coworking, provides insight into how creative work might be reimagined and practiced as learning encounters in search of alternatives to precarity.

Note

1 Established in 2016 but closed in 2021, Tate Exchange delivered themed programmes of arts projects that invited 'debate and reflect upon contemporary topics and ideas, get actively involved, think through doing, and make a difference' (Tate, n.d.)

References

Alacovska, A. (2020) 'From passion to compassion: A caring inquiry into creative work as socially engaged art', *Sociology*, 54(4), pp. 727–744. DOI: 10.1177/0038038520904716.

Belfiore, E. (2015) 'Impact, "value" and "bad economics": Making sense of the problem of value in the arts and humanities', *Arts & Humanities in Higher Education*, 14(1), pp. 95–110. DOI: 10.1177/1474022214531503.

Belfiore, E. (2021) 'Who cares? At what price? The hidden costs of socially engaged arts labour and the moral failure of cultural policy', *European Journal of Cultural Studies*, Online First. DOI: 10.1177/1367549420982863.

Benterrak, K., Muecke, S. and Roe, P. (1984/1996) *Reading the country*. South Freemantle, AU: Freemantle Arts Centre Press.

Beyes, T. and Michels, C. (2011) 'The production of educational space: Heterotopia and the business university', *Management Learning*, 42(5), pp. 521–536. https://doi.org/10.1177/1350507611400001.

Bishop, C. (2012) *Artificial Hells: Participatory art and the politics of spectatorship*. London: Verso.

Bissola, R., Imperatori, B. and Biffi, A. (2017) 'A rhizomatic learning process to create collective knowledge in entrepreneurship education: Open innovation and collaboration beyond boundaries', *Management Learning*, 48(2), pp. 206–226. https://doi.org/10.1177/1350507616672735.

Bureau, S.P. and Komporozos-Athanasiou, A. (2016) 'Learning subversion in the business school: An "improbable" encounter', *Management Learning*, 48(1), pp. 39–56. https://doi.org/10.1177/1350507616661262.

Butcher, T. (2021) 'Realising the meaning and value of online artist residencies during the pandemic', *blogpost*. Available at: https://es.britsoc.co.uk/realising-the-meaning-and-value-of-online-artist-residencies-during-the-pandemic/ (Accessed: 18 February 2023).

Colom, A. (2019) 'Who are we? – Open University REF impact study', *blogpost*. Available at: https://whoareweproject.com/ou-ref-impact-study (Accessed: 18 February 2023).

Cuddy-Keane, M. (2003) 'Defining cultural democracy: Modernism and universal individualism', *Key Words: A Journal of Cultural Materialism*, 4, pp. 56–77. Available at: www.jstor.org/stable/45367750.

Dowling, E. (2021) *The care crisis: What caused it and how we can end it?* London: Verso.

Finley, S., Vonk, C. and Finley, M.L. (2014) 'At home at school: Critical arts-based research as public pedagogy', *Cultural Studies ↔ Critical Methodologies*, 14(6), pp. 619–625. DOI: 10.1177/1532708614548134.

Freire, P. (1970) 'Cultural action and conscientization', *Harvard Educational Review*, 40(3), pp. 452–477. DOI: 10.17763/haer.40.3.h76250x720j43175.

Froggett, L., Little, R., Roy, A. and Whitaker, L. (2011) *New model visual arts organisations and social engagement*. Available at: http://clok.uclan.ac.uk/3024/1/WzW-NMI_Report%5B1%5D.pdf (Accessed: 2 February 2022).

Gramsci, A. (c.1933/1986) 'Prison notebooks', in Donald, J. and Hall, S. (eds.) *Politics and ideology*. Milton Keynes: Open University Press.

Hope, S. (2017) 'From community arts to the socially engaged art commission', in Jeffers, A. and Moriarty, G. (eds.) *Culture, democracy and the right to make art: The British community arts movement*. London: Bloomsbury Methuen Drama, pp. 203–222. DOI: 10.5040/9781474258395.ch-010.

Jeffers, A. (2017) 'Introduction', in Jeffers, A. and Moriarty, G. (eds.) *Culture, democracy and the right to make art: The British community arts movement*. London: Bloomsbury Methuen Drama, pp. 1–32. DOI: 10.5040/9781474258395.ch-001.

Kelly, O., Lock, J. and Merkel, K. (1986) *Cultural democracy: The manifesto, another standard*. London: Comedian Publishing. Available at: https://dibdibdob.com/stuffandbobs/culture-and-democracy.pdf (Accessed: 17 February 2023)

Kester, G. (2012) 'Conversation pieces: The role of dialogue in socially-engaged art', in Kocur, Z. and Leung, S. (eds.) *Theory in contemporary art since 1985*, 2nd edn. Hoboken, NJ: Blackwell, pp. 153–165.

Matarasso, F. (2019) *A restless art: How participation won, and why it matters*. London: Calouste Gulbenkian Foundation.

Mernick, A. (2021) 'Critical arts pedagogy: Nurturing critical consciousness and self-actualization through art education', *Art Education*, 74(5), pp. 19–24. DOI: 10.1080/00043125.2021.1928468.

Minestrelli, C. (2017) *Australian Indigenous hip hop: The politics of culture, identity and spirituality*. New York, NY: Routledge.

Minestrelli, C. (2020) 'New cityscapes: Redesigning urban cartographies through creative practices and critical pedagogies in London', in Storey, A.D., Sheehan, M. and Bodoh-Creed, J. (eds.) *The everyday life of urban inequality: Ethnographic case studies of global cities*. Lanham: Lexington Books, pp. 150–167. ISBN

9781793610645 (source). Available at: https://ualresearchonline.arts.ac.uk/id/eprint/15957/ (Accessed: 18 February 2023).

Mouffe, C. (2013) *Agonistics: Thinking the world politically.* London: Verso. eBook: eISBN 9781781682357.

O'Brien, Å. (2022) 'From the neighbourhood into the gallery: The ill-fitting Gresham wooden horse', *blogpost.* Available at: https://counterpointsarts.org.uk/from-the-neighbourhood-into-the-gallery-the-ill-fitting-gresham-wooden-horse/ (Accessed: 18 February 2023)

Probyn, E. (1996) *Outside belongings.* New York, NY: Routledge.

Reclaim the Archive. (n.d.) *Hip hop pedagogy and power: Reclaim the archive.* Available at: www.reclaimthearchive.com (Accessed: 18 February 2023).

Seth, A. (2021) *Being you: A new science of consciousness.* London: Faber & Faber.

Tate. (n.d.) *Tate exchange: 2016–2021.* Available at: www.tate.org.uk/tate-exchange (Accessed: 18 February 2023).

Who are we? (n.d.a) *About who are we?* Available at: https://whoareweproject.com/home-with-may-2019-programme/about-us (Accessed: 18 February 2023).

Who are we? (n.d.b) *As far as isolation goes.* Available at: https://whoareweproject.com/as-far-as-isolation-goes-2 (Accessed: 18 February 2023).

Who are we? (n.d.c) *Recognise – Risk – Reimagine – Rebuild – Redistribute.* Available at: https://whoareweproject.com/recognise-risk-reimagine-rebuild-redistribute-4 (Accessed: 18 February 2023).

Williams, R. (1961) *The long revolution.* London: Pelican Books.

Williams, R. (1980/2020) 'Beyond actually existing socialism', in Williams, R. (ed.) *Culture and materialism.* London: Verso, pp. 282–305.

Wright, D.E. (2020) 'Imagining a more just world: Critical arts pedagogy and youth participatory action research', *International Journal of Qualitative Studies in Education,* 33(1), pp. 32–49. DOI: 10.1080/09518398.2019.1678784.

6   Creating possibility

It's just work (not labour)

[The Job] is about a search, too, for daily meaning as well as daily bread, for recognition as well as cash, for astonishment rather than torpor; in short, for a sort of life rather than a Monday through Friday sort of dying. Perhaps immortality, too, is part of the quest.

(Terkel, 1974/2004, p. xi)

Here, Studs Terkel is talking about work not just as labour but as something that informs who we are. I say talking because reading his writing feels like he's telling it to me as it is. His observation is rooted in the everyday of hundreds of workers he interviewed, and that's why he is able to discuss work so matter-of-factly, so incisively. Terkel's accounts of what work means resonate with Raymond Williams' notion of a structure of feeling grounded in ordinary culture and class struggle. Work is so much more than what is individually traded as labour – it should be a life affirming collective cultural encounter filled with possibility; and if it doesn't feel that way, then we should do something about it.

This is what Chapters 4 and 5 have sought to show. Each case study points to curated collaborative learning experiences as a means through which to reimagine how and why creative work is done. In order to locate a structure of feeling within them, a significant amount of conceptualisation has been necessary through the book. Creative work is not as straightforward as the empty signifiers of creativity and precarity introduced in Chapter 1 would have us believe. Collaborative learning experiences don't just happen, nor do they necessarily free us from precarity. They are though a structured collectivist alternative to individualised striving and struggle. To unpack and make sense of this proposition, the theoretical connections made to develop the book's argument will be reconsidered.

As shown in Chapters 1 and 2, creative work is bound up in the ambiguities of creative economy discourse that conflate and confuse what we feel

DOI: 10.4324/9781003162025-6

in relation to work and life. We are constantly reminded that the world is uncertain, unstable and insecure, and we alone are responsible for working to free ourselves from the precarities of post-Fordism. Bayles and Orland, the authors that dare not use the dreaded C-word, suggest that 'uncertainty is the essential, inevitable and all-pervasive companion to your desire to make art. And tolerance for uncertainty is the pre-requisite for succeeding' (1993, p. 21). Such unhelpful meritocratic truisms feed off of the mythical notion of 'the struggling artist' and serve to convince us that the more individually creative we are the more economically successful we will become, and therefore the less individually precarious we will feel in the future. Yet what they actually do is remind us of our precarities in the present – that we are trapped in a Faustian bargain with the labour market. 'The reward for [good] work is more work,' as Tom Sachs suggests (van de Walle, n.d.).

The cunning ambiguity in Sachs' phrase could be interpreted as either an embrace of neoliberalism or a critique of it. It is indicative of Sachs' practice, but more substantively speaks to the self-regulating affective labour so many of us endure just to remain employable, as was discussed in Chapter 3. We pour our hearts and souls into our work, and for what? So few of us ever feel liberated from it, despite the promise of freedom. But what is freedom? Rather than freedom from labour, how does freedom to work on what truly matters to us sound? The practices discussed in Chapters 4 and 5 are filled with affective intensities that stem from injustices and intentionalities to do meaningful work, not to create surplus value. Work is not the problem; it's valorisation as labour is the issue.

And so, this book has sought to weave a way through the discursive entanglements of the creative economy to rediscover the ordinariness of work as a collaborative learning process in order to redirect attention away from the labour market, to instead find ways of working that are more meaningful to us and others. A light was shone on the problem of labour and discussed at length, not to go over the already well-trodden ground of political economy critique but to extract labour from our analyses in order to concentrate on locating work-based alternatives. As proposed in Chapter 1, the approach taken has been a rhizomatic one that has dug through disciplines ranging from sociology to philosophy, through political science, cultural studies and organisation studies, to make new conceptual and empirical connections in order to put down fresh roots. Hence, the working definition for creative work offered in Chapter 1 has been rendered obsolete, as was promised. Creative work is not bound to nor benefits from precarity. So, from these fresh roots, new collaborative creative work practices might be learned to propagate an alternative discourse – one that is less precarious and more ordinary; less economically driven and more culturally meaningful.

Learning to feel and act

In conceptually disassociating work from labour, our analyses have redirected the focus of creative work away from the labour market to the political; where the political is not politics per se, but the spaces in which we consider our relationships with politics (after Mouffe, 2013). Reimagining creative work in this way has opened up possibilities to contest the all-consuming current hegemony of creative economy discourse. We have not confronted the hegemony head on, but ventured into distinctly different spaces within the creative economy, with striking similarities, by following Chantal Mouffe's agonistic approach. For Mouffe, antagonism is fruitless; it works towards consensus that effectively maintains the status quo. Agonism though aims for dissensus, which holds radical possibilities for creating alternatives. As Raymond Williams has suggested, such an approach does though take an inordinate amount of time and effort (1980/2020). Agonistic politics chip away at the hegemony from within it. The case studies discussed reflect this. The discursive ambiguities of the creative economy are navigated in each context to do work that can be understood by both the market and the political. In coworking, there is an interplay between entrepreneurial and political intentionalities, while in socially engaged art, social inclusion ideals are translated into cultural democracy. As Derrida suggests, language is not fixed: 'every discourse is bricoleur' (1970/2014), and we can shift it.

To understand how, we have had to delve deeper conceptually. Mouffe suggests that agonistic acts are affective encounters, citing the work of individual artists as lenses through which publics are made sufficiently conscious of the current hegemony, to critically question it (2013). Through discrete artistic encounters, such as the *As far as isolation goes* installation discussed in Chapter 5, we can become viscerally engaged in the experience. By putting my arm through a hole in a wall at the *Who are We?* exhibition, I became immersed in a vulnerability that heightened my awareness of a specific political issue. This is not the easiest thing to understand conceptually, but if we consider such affective intensities to be pre-conscious bodily experience that we seek to make sense of (after Massumi, 2002), then we can see them as part of an embodied phenomenological process. What is shown in Chapters 4 and 5 is that in order to be sufficiently motivated to act on our felt experiences we must become conscious of how they make us feel and perhaps how others might feel in similar or more extreme situations. The embodied process of making conscious our affects and acting on them is phenomenologically understood as an intentionality that drives us towards taking action and gives meaning to sensation: 'Bodily intentionality brings the possibility of meaning into our experience' (Ménasé, in Merleau-Ponty, 2008, p. 9). Intentionality is the key to acting on what we feel.

So, if we find ourselves in a space filled with our own and others' affective intensities, then surely we will develop a heightened sense of shared intentionalities to act on them to such an extent that the collective will produced can topple the current hegemony. Not necessarily. The cunning of neoliberal logics is the appropriation of this embodied process – for example, we feel anxious and insecure, so we make sense of it as precarity, and typically act by working harder to remain employable, rather than working to contest it. Neoliberal discourses such as that of the creative economy are so pervasive, so consuming, so naturalised in everyday life that we need to (re)learn how to redirect our intentionalities if we are to refuse the hegemony and dissent. However, we have become so absorbed by individualising consumptive logics that few of us know how to act collectively towards dissensus. The idea that we live through perpetual crises keeps us so busy trying to fix them that rarely do we find the capacity to engage critically or act politically. There are of course many exceptions to this easily contestable rule of thumb, and thankfully it currently feels as if a new groundswell of direct participation is building in response to recent global crises, social injustices and misappropriations of political power. Yet, because we are so busy, so individualised and so responsiblised, we need to make time and space to (re)learn how to respond together and understand why we must.

In each of the cases discussed, learning encounters are curated to invite dialogues from which any number of possibilities might emerge. Curated collaborative learning encounters are therefore the key to giving structure to affective intensities, shared intentionalities and enacting them politically. Using Raymond Williams' terminology, curation draws out and gives a collective structure of feeling to affective intensities to produce possibilities that might otherwise remain individually untapped. In other words, by participating in collaborative learning experiences, we do not forget our precarities, but instead, we can harness our embodied experiences of them to raise our critical consciousness of their causes and debate how we might act to address them individually or collectively, entrepreneurially or politically. This process of learning to become critically conscious gives creative work meaning beyond labour. It is what can produce and practice possibility.

Helena is a visual storyteller, cultural producer and maker, with extensive experience as a professional curator. I first met Helena at a two-week urban photography summer school hosted at Goldsmiths College in London in 2018. Each day of the summer school was structured around aesthetic dialogue on-campus and unorthodox spatial encounters (photo-walks) in selected urban spaces, to invite critical engagements with urban geographies and foster collegial support and advice that encouraged the development of our individual photographic practices. Helena had travelled from Barcelona to participate in the summer school. I interviewed Helena in late 2019 and early 2020 after she had relocated to London.

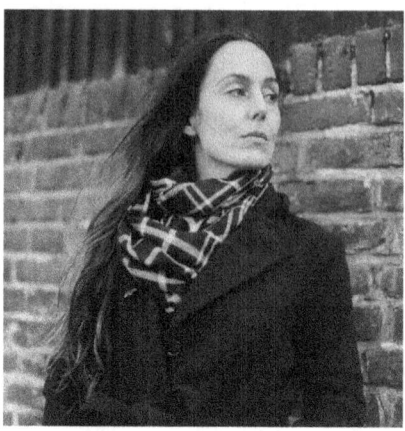

Image credit: Tim Butcher

'Learning has always been the key, any time I've felt stuck, I've felt a bit dead. Identifying the point where the learning process just stops it is our own responsibility in order to grow – to keep this process moving further.'

'Finding my own voice, doing whatever it is on my own terms and no one else's defines the search in my own practice. Articulating my narrative has something of having the feeling that it is me the one who is driving the car.'

'I got to the point where I got lost – Where am I? Where are we heading from here? What shall I do with all the cards I have? Is there any way I can make all of them useful to me and whoever this (familiar) other is?'

Creative work as bricolage

So, we can understand creative work as an embodied process of collaborative learning rather than something practiced precariously alone. Indeed, a common narrative of coworkers is that coworking spaces offer social connections that cannot be gained from working at home or in cafés, libraries and the like (Merkel, 2015). Melissa Gregg (2011) finds that remote working can affect us in profoundly unsettling ways. COVID-19 lockdown restrictions certainly confirmed this for many of us.

It would be easy to extend this discussion to a utopian conceptualisation of community as the ideal solution through which we might all learn to get along together. That idea has though already been deconstructed and de-mythologised (e.g. see Kanter, 1972). Rosabeth Moss Kanter shows how while communes can provide alternatives to everyday life that offer hopeful escapism, they are typically short-lived (1972). Their initial vitalities become institutionalised, routinised and obscured with each new generation (Kanter, 1972). This was something I witnessed in coworking, and hence why I refer to it mostly in the past tense. As the space I coworked in the most expanded, membership grew and new ventures took flight, successful early protagonists moved on and their vibrant ways of working proved difficult to replicate (Butcher, 2018). So, there is at least something to be said for ephemerality in learning encounters. Series of discrete learning projects that build on each other as shown in the socially engaged arts cases is perhaps preferable in order to inject fresh vitality into iterative encounters, rather than attempting to hold groups together as a community.

More directly relevant to what this book aims to achieve, Jean Lave finds that 'when the organisation of work practice (e.g. "communities of practice") is imposed from the top down it strips the concept of its critical character' (2019, p. 143). Lave scathingly calls out how the communities of practice model has been utilised by institutions to reinforce the current hegemony:

> It was taken up from corporate and educational establishment positions of power and drew lessons about management organization, possibilities for commoditised knowledge production and mandated creativity, encouraged in the belief that it would foster 'regional economic drivers' and 'incubators of entrepreneurship.'
>
> (2019, p. 143)

Hence, besides ephemerality, the ambiguity and irreducibility of complex intersubjectivities in collaborative learning encounters might enable them to resist institutionalising logics and lean into counter-hegemonic dissent. The radical elusiveness of legitimate peripheral participation, as opposed to the static communities of practice model, is that it is universally practicable, easily understood when observed or practiced, but invariably difficult to put into language and thereby potentially irreducible to a specific series of replicable activities to achieve a pre-determined outcome. Legitimate peripheral participation is situational, relational and emergent. Every learning encounter is unique, and what is learned in one encounter can be passed on to and adapted by others. It is a thoroughly creative way of working.

From the perspective of cultural materialism (Williams, 1980/2020), what is it that is generative of the sorts of affective experiences found in the collaborative learning encounters discussed so far? The common theme running through the case studies is bricolage. Each of the learning encounters studied has been discussed in terms of the symbolic interactions and materialities in particular spaces. In socially engaged arts projects, the making of art together provides the aesthetic third necessary to foster dialogue (Froggett *et al.*, 2011; Kester, 2012). In coworking, modular, movable objects and permission to reorganise them invite ideation (Butcher, 2018). There is a DIY aesthetic in each case – a 'roaming through culturally meaningful artefacts to pick up useful bits and pieces to repair and improve', that Benterrak, Muecke and Roe define (1984/1996, p. 168). Each encounter and its outcomes are determined by what is brought to the table, so to speak. There is a vitality in the bricolage of ordinary interactions that elicits the affective responses that might generate intentionalities. 'Bricolage becomes visible when we can *trace* the origins of the different pieces making up the whole' (Benterrak, Muecke and Roe, 1984/1996, p. 168, emphasis in original). So rather than seeking to escape ordinary everyday things, they are embraced, as Raymond Williams suggests (1980/2020). Things that might otherwise be considered mundane, familiar and unremarkable, or routine, repetitive and rhythmic can be reimagined as creative, adaptive and defiant (Scott, 2009). This is the power of bricolage. It is a universal cultural practice that can prove to be both individually fulfilling and collectively meaningful, while remaining uniquely situational, emergent and like legitimate peripheral participation difficult for the market to appropriate. From men's sheds to punk, bricolage can invite dialogue that enables us to identify who we are and what we are free to do (after Williams, 1978/1989).

As a form of cultural expression, bricolage therefore gives specificity to each experience of it. Within collaborative learning encounters, bricolage is arguably what generates specific meaningful outcomes. The Gresham Wooden Horse discussed in Chapter 5 is a good example of this. The collaborative acts of making the large-scale wooden horse were generative of cross-cultural dialogue that not only co-produced a neighbourhood plan but also opened up opportunities for mutual care and support. Bayles and Orland have something quite enlightening to say about this phenomenon: 'what we really gain from the artmaking of others is courage-by-association. Depth of contact grows as fears are shared – and thereby disarmed – and this comes from embracing art as process, and artists as kindred spirits. To the artist, art is a verb' (1993, p. 90). Ordinary acts of bricolage create cultural possibilities, not market opportunities.

In fact, it is arguable that legitimate peripheral participation combined with bricolage circulate possibility. That is to say that by being such accessible and ordinary practices, they can be practiced however, wherever and whenever, as often as we'd like. Each time we practice bricolage, as Benterrak, Muecke and Roe (1984/1996) allude to, we draw on prior cultural artefacts to make new ones. So, when employed in collaborative learning encounters that involve practical acts of making, repair and improvement, new possibilities can be explored. So, if creative work is experienced as practice-based collaborative learning, its ephemerality, ambiguity and irreducibility might resist economic valorisation, create practical alternatives to current understandings of what and who work should be for, and yet retain its ordinariness and vitality.

Cultural democracy and meaningful work

Farhad is a socially engaged artist and creative professional. His working practices span photography, graphic design and other associated creative processes. Not unlike Selina in Chapter 1, Farhad finds ways to balance commercial and artistic projects. Both types of work are meaningful to him; each is part of a learning process, as he suggests.

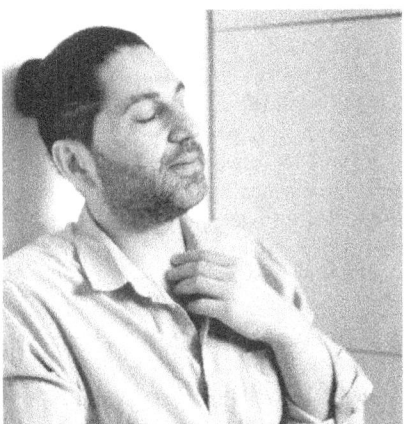

Image credit: Tim Butcher

'It is all about the process. The final thing doesn't matter that much. It's what we learn through it.'
    'My work talks about myself, it's about my journey. When you are making art about yourself, it is more meaningful.'

The argument developed through the book does not lead to an obvious solution to precarity. There is no model that can reduce creative work to a series of rational steps leading to a precarity-free life. Instead, something more meaningful is drawn out, something that might enable us to slip from the grip of our Faustian bargains, at least from time to time, if not permanently. What is proposed is that we find ways to work within in the creative economy to agonistically chip away at its hegemony without it noticing. The process of producing and practicing possibility is what is important, not what we produce for the market, but through creative work we should be able to do both.

We have seen that ambiguities in the discourse can unwittingly enable dissent. Hidden in plain sight, we can use its rhetoric to play with the discourse and seek out alternatives. Coworking, for example, can be used to build the support structures – structures of feeling – that enterprising creatives need to bricolage and test out their new ideas and unorthodox identities. Meanwhile, in arts work, cultural democracy can be produced while also meeting the aim of social inclusion. As argued in Chapter 5, cultural democracy is not the antithesis of social inclusion but perhaps its critical conscience. Equally, creative work can choose to move between or meld together entrepreneurial and political intentionalities; and neither need be antagonistic nor ask for consent. Neither coworking or socially engaged art participate in the politics of disturbance, but instead, bricolage learning practices to co-create interconnected counter-hegemonic acts (after Mouffe, 2013).

It is possible to be both entrepreneurial and artistic. Today, these are not mutually exclusive fixed identities; the market has seen to that. And so, we must find ways to adapt our creative work to pay the bills *and* ensure it remains meaningful. However, if we do so alone, it won't be easy. If we can (re)learn how to practice together, we open up far more possibilities. This is why collaborative learning encounters hold the key to reimagining creative work: a groundswell of shared affective intensities holds far more potential to reimagine work and life beyond precarity than if we struggle on alone.

There are perhaps three ideas you might take away from this book. The first being the social process of learning to work collaboratively and the second being the cultural materialities of unorthodox learning encounters. The third, I had not anticipated when I began this project. It is that while many complex concepts developed by theorists from a range of fields have been brought together here, the one scholar I have been most inspired by has been Raymond Williams. Like me, you too might find his ideas on learning, culture and direct participation still relevant today, and maybe more than ever.

Stuart Hall has noted that Williams' interest is in the whole experience of life in a specific place with all its complexities, and in doing so he developed many contestable arguments and concepts (1983/2016). His notion of ordinariness is something that Richard Hoggart (1957/1962) saw as nostalgic for a mythical past, for instance. However, while Williams' writing is often considered difficult to dissect (Hall, 1983/2016), it stems from a frustration with colleagues and students he encountered at Cambridge University who had little if any consideration for the sort of ordinary everyday life and work he experienced growing up and living in the rural village of Llanvihangel Crucorney on the Welsh border with England (after Large Door, 1988). For Williams, ordinariness is very real. It is founded on a desire for cultural democracy, learned through straightforward encounters in the everyday, enacted as keen observations of inequalities and social injustices, and put to work through public scholarship. Today there are many academics engaged in the everyday but so few enact critical consciousness as public scholarship in the ways that Williams did. The popular media is more invested in distracting us than engaging us in critique. So, instead, we tend to turn to social influencers and innovators rather than academics for insight into how they navigate work and life.

If Williams were an academic today, he might well be sharing his ideas through YouTube and podcasts rather than via books and television, but he would not be doing so uncritically. As suggested in the quote at the beginning of this book, culture is ordinary, but that does not mean we should take it for granted. By locating the ordinariness of creative work, we can develop a critical consciousness of everything it is not but which the market would have us believe it is. Creative work need not be precarious, but instead should be something we can all find meaningful. Only together can we remind ourselves of this.

Epilogue: learning together

> Democratic egalitarianism has one source in the assumption that all are of equal worthiness in a much more valuable sense; overweening freedom owes much to the idea that we must try to be responsible for our own fate and decisions; . . . Yet the problem is acute and pressing – how that freedom may be kept as in any sense a meaningful thing whilst the processes of centralisation and technological development continue.
>
> (Hoggart, 1957/1962, p. 345)

Not unlike Williams, Richard Hoggart's concern is for us all to feel and act, live and work in culturally meaningful ways. They each saw how such freedoms were being taken over (see also Williams, 1961). In the post-war years of mid-twentieth century Britain, they witnessed progressive educational reforms that offered a comprehensive education to an increasing number of working-class people. They also experienced the introduction of television, and Williams particularly saw it as a means through which to reimagine culture and encourage direct political participation. It was a pivotal time, at least in Britain, when through increased access to knowledge, the critical consciousness of the working classes was heightened. A radical reimagining of culture, society and what we are each free (and not free) to do became possible. However, Hoggart's concerns about how we interpret and enact freedom were borne out as neoliberalism appropriated the egalitarian pursuit of universal individualism – it turned ideas about work towards equal human rights (Cuddy-Keane, 2003) into marketable individualised meritocratic ideals. The architects of neoliberalism sought not only to deregulate industry and privatise public services, but also to dismantle any sort of collective resistance to the hegemony they were building by distracting us with individualising pursuits.

Desire and affect are central to the human experience. They well up preconsciously and can be made conscious critically or uncritically. So, to feel free from hegemony is not a battle of wills, but a confrontation between desires (after Balibar, 1985/2008). Here Balibar uses Spinoza's definition of desire as: 'both to the individual's effort to preserve his [sic] own being (his [sic] own form) and to the peculiarly human consciousness of this effort' (1985/2008, p. 105). If we are to free creative work from precarity we must consciously contest our desires for the trappings of neoliberal capitalism.

As discussed, those trappings are not though easy to distinguish. Only through unorthodox yet ordinary collaborative learning encounters can we strip away the distractions and share the knowledge and experience necessary to develop our critical consciousness of precarity and our intentionalities to contest it. The more opportunities we have to learn with and from each other, the more we might hone our criticality, to see through the ambiguities and bricolage them to make the most of what freedoms we have.

Education in schools and universities has been swallowed up by market logics and neoliberal ideals. Much of contemporary education promotes the orthodox consumptive ideals that neoliberalism requires us to believe in. There is little time or space for criticality or dissent. So, instead, the sorts of unorthodox, hidden-in-plain-sight collaborative learning encounters discussed in this book are where our affects and desires are most likely to be drawn out and our critically conscious intentionalities realised. As Raymond Williams suggests, we need more such ordinary everyday critical encounters. We need more unorthodox experiences, more opportunities to bricolage and more mutuality and conviviality in order to share and learn from well-founded ideas and contemporary cultural experiences. Only by working to create alternative learning encounters can we feel free to begin to imagine new possibilities.

References

Balibar, E. (1985/2008) *Spinoza and politics*. Translated by Snowdon, P. London: Verso.

Bayles, D. and Orland, T. (1993) *Art and fear: Observations on the perils (and rewards) of artmaking*. Sacramento, CA: Image Continuum.

Benterrak, K., Muecke, S. and Roe, P. (1984/1996) *Reading the country*. South Freemantle, AU: Freemantle Arts Centre Press.

Butcher, T. (2018) 'Learning everyday entrepreneurial practices through coworking', *Management Learning*, 49(3), pp. 327–345. https://doi.org/10.1177/1350507618757088.

Cuddy-Keane, M. (2003) 'Defining cultural democracy: Modernism and universal individualism', *Key Words: A Journal of Cultural Materialism*, 4, pp. 56–77. Available at: www.jstor.org/stable/45367750.

Derrida, J. (1970/2014) 'Structure, sign and play in the discourse of the human sciences', in Lodge, D. and Wood, N. (eds.) *Modern criticism and theory: A reader*. New York, NT: Routledge.

Froggett, L., Little, R., Roy, A. and Whitaker, L. (2011) *New model visual arts organisations and social engagement*. Available at: http://clok.uclan.ac.uk/3024/1/WzW-NMI_Report%5B1%5D.pdf (Accessed: 2 February 2022).

Gregg, M. (2011) *Work's intimacies*. Cambridge: Polity Press.

Hall, S. (1983/2016) 'Lecture 2: Culturalism', in Daryl Slack, J. and Grossberg, L. (eds.) *Cultural studies 1983: A theoretical history*. Durham, NC: Duke University Press, pp. 25–53.

Hoggart, R. (1957/162) *The uses of literacy: Aspects of working-class life with special reference to publications and entertainments*. Harmondsworth: Penguin Books.

Kanter, R.M. (1972) *Commitment and community: Communes and utopias in sociological perspective*. Cambridge, MA: Harvard University Press.

Kester, G. (2012) 'Conversation pieces: The role of dialogue in socially-engaged art', in Kocur, Z. and Leung, S. (eds.) *Theory in contemporary art since 1985*, 2nd edn. Hoboken, NJ: Blackwell, pp. 153–165.

Large Door. (1988) *Raymond Williams: A tribute*, a film for Channel 4 (Dir. Coutts, D.). Available at: www.youtube.com/watch?v=rcgmUOF4hUI&list=PLRNiv2HKEUXF sGW5pt6sJNQuGmBx3u1YX&index=34 (Accessed: 22 February 2022).

Lave, J. (2019) *Learning and everyday life: Access, participation, and changing practice*. Cambridge: Cambridge University Press.

Massumi, B. (2002) *Parables for the virtual: Movement, affect, sensation*. Durham, NC: Duke University Press.

Ménasé, S. (2008) 'Foreword', in Merleau-Ponty, M. (ed.) *The world of perception*. Abingdon: Routledge, pp. vii–viii.

Merkel, J. (2015) 'Coworking in the city', *Ephemera: Theory and Politics in Organization*, 15(1), pp. 121–139. Available at: https://ephemerajournal.org/contribution/coworking-city.

Mouffe, C. (2013) *Agonistics: Thinking the world politically*. London: Verso. eBook: eISBN 9781781682357.

Scott, S. (2009) *Making sense of everyday life*. Cambridge: Polity Press.

Terkel, S. (1974/2004) *Working: People talk about what they do all day and how they feel about what they do*. New York, NY: The New Press.

van de Walle, M. (n.d.) *Tom Sachs: Biography*. Available at: www.tomsachs.com/biography (Accessed: 17 February 2023).

Williams, R. (1961) *The long revolution*. London: Pelican Books.

Williams, R. (1978/1989) 'Art: Freedom as duty', in Gable, R. (ed.) *Resources of hope*. London: Verso, pp. 88–95.

Williams, R. (1980/2020) 'Beyond actually existing socialism', in Williams, R. (ed.) *Culture and materialism*. London: Verso, pp. 282–305. Previously published in New Left Review, 120, March–April 1980.

Appendix – research methods

Seeing, listening and participating

> Sociology's future, at least its immediate future, lies in an effort to reincarnate and to re-establish itself as *cultural politics in the service of human freedom*.
>
> (Bauman, 2011, p. 170)

There are many labels applied to social science research to distinguish and articulate its many approaches, but in doing so we should not lose sight of why we do it. I am a visual ethnographer interested in our relationships with work (so, a sociologist of work too). The methods I use aim to understand how we make sense of those relationships (see Butcher, 2013). The problem that Zygmunt Bauman points to is what lends criticality to my approach.

As this book has shown, the lines between work and freedom have been blurred. Too many of us experience work as a means to an end, and not everyone has access to fair and equitable working conditions. Yet work is a cultural encounter through which we define ourselves (Terkel, 1974/2004). Through meaningful work, we can understand who we are and what we are free to do (Williams, 1978/1989). So, this is a sociological study of creative work that employs a range of methods from different research projects to understand how we might reimagine work as something less precarious and more culturally significant.

This is a multimodal study (Höllerer, Jancsary and Grafström, 2018) that interprets texts, observations and participations in coworking, socially engaged art and the wider creative economy. It seeks to account for discourses, intersubjectivities, relationalities, embodiments and affects, to show how creative work is informed by how we talk about it, how we enact it, who we do that with, and how that makes us feel. This study is in many ways a bricolage itself (Cunliffe, 2003). It is predominantly a reflexive hermeneutic study (Cunliffe, 2011) of shared experiences that interprets participants' experiences and my own, and frames them within what we already understand about the creative economy to draw out critical insights. It also employs geneology to understand how the creative economy came into being and how it has been shaped by ideology (after Tamboukou, 1999; Garland, 2014), to give context to the empirical findings from my research into coworking (2012–14) and socially engaged art (2018–20).

The coworking research is ethnographic in the poststructuralist sense of being both participant observation and observer participation, where I (the observer) both observed other coworkers and actively participated in coworking (see Butcher, 2013, 2018). This longitudinal, immersive approach enabled me to not only learn from others' experiences but also my own. I listened, observed and got involved in learning how to cowork. I coworked intermittently but worked at one particular space – sometimes two or three times a week – regularly enough to get involved in and organise social and learning events. Being so immersed, I needed to be mindful of my own reflexivities. I could not remove myself from the research and so I ensured I accounted for my own encounters and my intersubjectivities with other participants (Butcher, 2013). The coworking case (and those of socially engaged art) are narrated in the first person. Maintaining a critical distance is never easy in such immersive research. The affective vitalities (after Bell and Vachhani, 2020) of coworking drew me in and it was long after the empirical work was completed and I'd engaged with other studies of coworking that I was able to reflect critically on the phenomenon as a whole and conceptualise it as a learning process (see Butcher, 2018).

My insights into socially engaged art are from a more nuanced series of approaches rather than a single ethnography. My interest in this phenomenon began as the *Tales of Precarity* research project that produced the visual stories from which the vignettes throughout the book stem from. My initial interest was in precarious work, which had been sparked by both encounters with coworkers and my research with the people of Papunya in central Australia on a project called *Wellbeing not Winning* (2015–18), which for my part sought to understand the meaning and vitality of sporting participation for communities with few opportunities to engage in paid labour. It was in that project that I began using photographic methods (see Butcher, Hallinan and Judd, 2016).

For *Tales of Precarity,* I developed a visual storytelling methodology based on the well-founded photo elicitation approach (see Harper, 1987/1992). In short, my approach is to interview individual participants, record the audio from our dialogues and photograph them as they share with me details of their life worlds (Brown *et al.*, 2011) and I observe the social poetics of their practices (Cunliffe, 2002). This data collection process is repeated at least once, with subsequent interviews using photo-elicitation to show participants the images I've made along with transcriptions of recorded audio, and asking them what meaning they might make from them and what they might have been feeling in those moments. It is both a way to co-curate their stories and explore whether the combination of photographic images and transcribed spoken words can bring affective experiences (e.g. precarity) into consciousness. Experiences that might otherwise remain pre-conscious (after Massumi, 2002) or be difficult to discuss without visual or textual cues. Methodologically, I purposefully use analogue photography; developing the film and printing the images myself in the darkroom. The materialities produce a multi-layered immersive experience that deepens my inquiries with participants, and in turn fosters the trust, dialogue and shared understandings necessary to co-curate their visual stories. The vignettes presented through this book, are excerpts of stories from that project, which I interpret as being especially relevant to the subject of the chapter they each feature in.

Otherwise, my experiences of socially engaged art have been as an observer and participant, not as complete ethnographies but as a bricolage of various encounters that I was involved in to some extent. In effect, I learned about the organisation, pedagogies and practices of socially engaged art through legitimate peripheral participation (Lave, 1991) – reflexively practicing what I preach. Being commissioned by Counterpoints Arts, *Tales of Precarity* gave me access to some of the planning and organisation of the 2019 *Who are We?* exhibition, and through my own sense of commitment to project participants and interest in the wider body of work, I visited the exhibition and participated as discussed in Chapter 5 on each of its five days. Not unlike in coworking, I made social connections through which I felt a desire to give something back (after Mauss, 1990/1925, cited in Scott, 2009).

For *Reclaim the Archive*, I was a member of the project team, meeting in person with other team members in late 2019 and January 2020. From March 2020, we regularly met online to reshape the project in line with COVID-19 restrictions, support the artists through their residencies and work with the designers commissioned to produce the project website. In referring to this project, I draw solely on the publicly available artefacts published on its website (see Reclaim the Archive, n.d.). Due to my relocation from London to Tasmania in March 2020, I was very much on the periphery of the project. Also, the extreme uncertainties, insecurities and instabilities of everyone's situations at that time meant that I was very well aware of the constraints on our reflexivities and relationalities. So, I chose not to collect empirical data.

Otherwise, I encounter shared working arrangements, socially engaged art and the global creative economy more generally throughout my life. I visit art galleries, watch creators on YouTube, work alongside entrepreneurs, meet freelancers and have friends that run start-ups, creative ventures and arts studios. I do not collect data from them, but as shown through this book, I reflect on the pervasiveness of the creative economy, its discourses and all of my own entanglements with it. Overall, my ontology and axiology are indicative of the phenomena I research. My research practice is a form of situated learning through which I get involved in the processes I seek to understand and with that comes a responsibility (Butcher, 2013).

Ethics, self and other

Drought refugees from Oklahoma camping by the roadside. They hope to work in the cotton fields. There are seven in the family. Blythe, California, 1936.

(Lange, 1936/2014, p. 32)

Perhaps one of the greatest documentarians of precarity is Dorothea Lange. While *Migrant Mother* is Lange's most recognisable work, her contribution to photography is arguably unparalleled in representing the affects of uncertainty, instability and insecurity. The aforementioned quotation is the title of another of Lange's photographs for the Farm Security Administration (FSA), which documented the movement of ordinary families towards California in search of work, displaced by the dust bowl that devastated the Great Plains of the US in the 1930s. The image associated with the title is of a man with his head in his weathered hands, laying on his chest in the foreground, and a woman behind nursing a small child under a makeshift tarpaulin. Linda Gordon (2014, p. 32), notes that 'Lange did not much like the image because it rendered these people as victims, their mood one of hopelessness, and because the woman appears simpleminded [sic].' Lange's self-reflexive ethic of care is something I seek to always emulate in my own work. I see myself as the custodian of the images that research participants allow me to make and the stories they share with me.

I could list many influences that inform my sense of custodianship. In an article published in 2013, I begin to make sense of it as being constituted in my formative experiences of legitimate peripheral participation, and as a sense of connection to work and workers based on my own working-class origins (see Butcher, 2013). Ethnography is for me more than a method, it is an ontology – a way of experiencing the cultural totality of a place. Perhaps this is why I relate to Raymond Williams' work.

More recently, I learned a great deal from working with the people of Papunya on the *Wellbeing not Winning project* in central Australia. With little said, I learned to listen and to see. The cultural vitalities of sporting participation were not easy to translate (nor should they be) but I was fortunate to see them in plain sight once I had attuned to their cultural materialities (see Butcher and Judd, 2016). I learned also why they should not be translated or decoded. Although I was welcomed by community members and given permission to observe, photograph and ask questions, their stories are not mine to tell (Wright, 2016). This is why I developed a method of co-curating visual stories and why I continue to refine it. Doing the research and writing this book is how I learn about my own relationship with work, life and hegemony. Co-curation and custodianship are how make sense of the research I do.

Overall, my research approach is founded on mutuality and trust. I learn from people inviting me into their lives and us sharing our practices, so that I can not only understand how they make sense of their experiences of work, life and precarity, but also come to terms with my own. Yes, precarity is something I feel and I want to understand why and how to overcome it. I do appreciate my privileges and also the disadvantages so many people in the world face. Many people feel far more precarious than me and do not have the same opportunities to reflect or act on it as I do. And I acknowledge that this book is founded on research situated in the Global North, but I hope that its basic argument is trustworthy and has some universality, so it might be applied more broadly.

References

Bauman, Z. (2011) *Collateral damage: Social inequalities in a global age.* Cambridge: Polity Press.

Bell, E. and Vachhani, S.J. (2020) 'Relational encounters and vital materiality in the practice of craft work', *Organization Studies*, 41(5), pp. 681–701. https://doi.org/10.1177/0170840619866482.

Brown, S.D., Cromby, J., Harper, D.J., Johnson, K. and Reavey, P. (2011) 'Researching "experience": Embodiment, methodology, process', *Theory & Psychology*, 21(4), pp. 493–515. https://doi.org/10.1177/0959354310377543.

Butcher, T. (2013), Longing to belong', *Qualitative Research in Organizations and Management*, 8(3), pp. 242–257. https://doi.org/10.1108/QROM-05-2012-1065.

Butcher, T. (2018) 'Learning everyday entrepreneurial practices through coworking', *Management Learning*, 49(3), pp. 327–345. https://doi.org/10.1177/1350507618757088.

Butcher, T., Hallinan, C. and Judd, B. (2016) 'Traversing ontological dispositions: The intersection between remote Indigenous communities and elite urban-based men's football organisation', in Molnar, G. and Purdy, L. (eds.) *Ethnographies in sport and exercise research.* Abingdon: Routledge, pp. 165–180.

Butcher, T. and Judd, B. (2016) 'The aboriginal football ethic: Where the rules get flexible', *Griffith Review*, 53, pp. 167–176. ISSN 1839–2954.

Cunliffe, A.L. (2002) 'Social poetics as management inquiry: A dialogical approach', *Journal of Management Inquiry*, 11(2), pp. 128–146. https://doi.org/10.1177/10592602011002006.

Cunliffe, A.L. (2003) 'Reflexive inquiry in organizational research: Questions and possibilities', *Human Relations*, 56(8), pp. 983–1003. https://doi.org/10.1177/00187267030568004.

Cunliffe, A.L. (2011) 'Crafting qualitative research: Morgan and smircich 30 years on', *Organizational Research Methods*, 14(4), pp. 647–673. https://doi.org/10.1177/1094428110373658.

Garland, D. (2014) 'What is a "history of the present"? On Foucault's genealogies and their critical preconditions', *Punishment & Society*, 16(4), pp. 365–384. https://doi.org/10.1177/1462474514541711.

Gordon, L. (ed.) (2014) *Aperture masters of photography: Dorothea Lange.* New York, NY: Aperture Foundation.

Harper, D. (1987/1992) *Working knowledge: Skill and community in a small shop.* Berkley, CA: University of California Press.

Höllerer, M.A., Jancsary, D. and Grafström, M. (2018) 'A picture is worth a thousand words': Multimodal sensemaking of the global financial crisis', *Organization Studies*, 39(5–6), pp. 617–644. https://doi.org/10.1177/0170840618765019.

Lange, D. (1936/2014) 'Drought refugees from Oklahoma camping by the roadside. They hope to work in the cotton fields, there are seven in the family. Blythe, California', in Gordon, L. (ed.) *Aperture masters of photography: Dorothea Lange.* New York, NY: Aperture Foundation.

Lave, J. (1991) 'Situated learning in communities of practice', in Resnick, L.B., Levine, J.M. and Teasley, S.D. (eds.) *Perspectives on socially shared cognition.* Washington, DC: American Psychological Association, pp. 63–82.

Massumi, B. (2002) *Parables for the virtual: Movement, affect, sensation.* Durham, NC: Duke University Press.

Reclaim the Archive. (n.d.) *Hip hop pedagogy and power: Reclaim the archive.* Available at: www.reclaimthearchive.com (Accessed: 18 February 2023).

Scott, S. (2009) *Making sense of everyday life.* Cambridge: Polity Press.

Tamboukou, M. (1999) 'Writing genealogies: An exploration of Foucault's strategies for doing research', *Discourse Studies in the Cultural Politics of Education*, 20(2), pp. 201–217. DOI: 10.1080/0159630990200202.

Terkel, S. (1974/2004) *Working: People talk about what they do all day and how they feel about what they do.* New York, NY: The New Press.

Williams, R. (1978/1989) 'Art: Freedom as duty', in Gable, R. (ed.) *Resources of hope.* London: Verso, pp. 88–95.

Wright, A. (2016) 'What happens when you tell somebody else's story?' *Meanjin Quarterly*, Summer. Available at: https://meanjin.com.au/essays/what-happens-when-you-tell-somebody-elses-story/ (Accessed: 18 February 2023).

Index

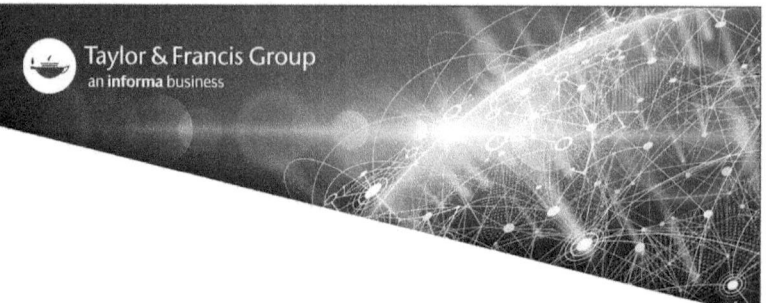
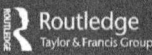
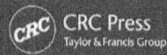

For Product Safety Concerns and Information please contact our EU
representative GPSR@taylorandfrancis.com
Taylor & Francis Verlag GmbH, Kaufingerstraße 24, 80331 München, Germany